The Complete Guide to Poochons

Candace Darnforth

LP Media Inc. Publishing
Text copyright © 2021 by LP Media Inc.
All rights reserved.

No part of this book may be reproduced or transmitted in any form or by any means, electronic or mechanical, including photocopying, recording, or by an information storage and retrieval system – except by a reviewer who may quote brief passages in a review to be printed in a magazine or newspaper – without permission in writing from the publisher.
For information address LP Media Inc. Publishing, 3178 253rd Ave. NW, Isanti, MN 55040

www.lpmedia.org

Publication Data

Candace Darnforth

The Complete Guide to Poochons – First edition.

Summary: "Successfully raising a Poochon Dog from puppy to old age" – Provided by publisher.

ISBN: 978-1-954288-14-0

[1. Poochons – Non-Fiction] I. Title.

This book has been written with the published intent to provide accurate and authoritative information in regard to the subject matter included. While every reasonable precaution has been taken in preparation of this book the author and publisher expressly disclaim responsibility for any errors, omissions, or adverse effects arising from the use or application of the information contained inside. The techniques and suggestions are to be used at the reader's discretion and are not to be considered a substitute for professional veterinary care. If you suspect a medical problem with your dog, consult your veterinarian.
Design by Sorin Rădulescu
First paperback edition, 2021
Cover Photo Courtesy of Steven Higham - @poochongeorge on Instagram

TABLE OF CONTENTS

INTRODUCTION

Tiny, fluffy, cuddly, intelligent, low-shedding and loyal? What more could you ask for in a dog?

The Poochon is a bundle of love in an adorable, curly, little package! Poochons have become one of the most popular designer dog breeds,

Photo Courtesy of Angela Marshall

thanks to their sunny personalities and their desire to please their owners. The hardest part about being a Poochon pet owner is not being able to take your dog for a walk without strangers asking to pat your handsome puppy.

Poochons inherited the friendly, sociable nature of the Bichon and the intelligence of the Poodle, making them ideal companions for you and your family. The Poochon's lovable appearance will steal your heart instantly, with its big brown eyes and droopy ears. It is hard to find another canine which tries harder than the Poochon to please a beloved owner. Your dog will want to be by your side at all times and will thrive on your love and attention.

If you are considering a Poochon, this book will introduce you to their personality traits and everything you need to know about caring for your dog from day one. No matter how fun and easy-going the Poochon is, you need to know loads of information before you bring your new four-pawed buddy home.

Poochons make excellent therapy dogs and life-long companions. They quickly adapt to new situations and can be trained to do just about anything. The only thing your Poochon cannot learn is something you did not teach him. In this book, you will learn how to use positive reinforcement in training your Poochon to do what is expected of him in different circumstances, and so much more.

Bringing a new dog into your home is a big responsibility, but this book is a gold-mine of tips and tricks to help you create a life-long bond between you and your pet. You will learn what your Poochon needs to be a healthy and happy dog, long into his senior years.

So, without further ado, continue reading to embark on your exciting journey with your new best friend!

CHAPTER 1

Meet the Poochon

Poochons are gentle and sociable, not to mention cute, from their soft, floppy ears right down to their ever-wagging tails. Not only are these pups considered to be one of the cutest designer breeds in the world, but they are also some of the friendliest, happiest and most loyal of all dogs.

Photo Courtesy of Jayne Dixon

FUN FACT
How Popular Are They?

Poochons have been around for at least 30 years and originated in Australia in the 1990s. According to the polling website Dogell, Poochons are ranked 560th in popularity out of 623 breeds overall as of 2021. Hybrid dogs have become increasingly popular in recent years, and this breed's popularity may grow as this trend continues.

The Poochon's rambunctious personality and love is contagious, spreading laughter and smiles to everyone they meet. They are often described as real-life teddy bears who love to cuddle with their families. Your Poochon's happiness depends on the simple things in life, such as a short walk, a belly rub or a snuggle on the sofa.

Coming home to a Poochon is never lonely, with a bundle of fluff running excitedly towards you, simply because you finally made it back home to them.

What Makes the Poochon Different?

The Poochon is a cross between a purebred Toy Poodle and a Bichon Frise, resulting in a small, affectionate, and adorable canine. Poochons are considered to be part of the popular "doodle" mix family. They are also known as Bichpoo, Bichon Poodle Mix or Bichon Poo. They have floppy ears, a pointy nose, and dark, brown eyes.

Poochons need to be socialized at an early age, as they tend to become nervous or aggressive in unfamiliar situations or while meeting an unfamiliar dog or person. When properly socialized, Poochons make excellent companions for large families with children or for single households. They do not thrive in homes where they will be left alone for long periods of time. Poochons easily adapt to different living spaces, such as apartment buildings or a house with a backyard. All they need is a human family nearby.

Poochons thrive on the company of human companions and are always up for a game, an excuse to show their love and affection or simply to be the center of attention - often, all at the same time! It is almost impossible to look down at your smiling Poochon and not smile back.

Poochons are a low-shedding dog and are considered to be hypo-allergenic. However, Poochons still have dander - a common allergen. No dog is completely hypo- allergenic.

Their medium-length coat requires extra grooming and maintenance because they do not shed their hair seasonally. If your dog's coat is not

Photo Courtesy of
Kayla-Jade Harrison

regularly brushed, it can easily become matted or form knots which are difficult to remove. Once every six weeks, you will need to give your Poochon a bath and trim your pet's toenails.

Poochons require moderate exercise. Of course, they love going for walks and playing fetch in the park just as much as most dogs. They have lots of energy to burn off and require about thirty minutes of exercise daily, preferably outside. Even though Poochons are sociable, playful, and cuddly dogs, they can be very stubborn. This can be a challenge while training them.

What is a Designer Dog?

Hybrid dogs or designer dogs are a cross between two different purebred breeds.

A purebred dog comes from generations of selective breeding from the same breed. Purebred dogs are preferred by many pet owners because this means that they know what they are getting. Every purebred puppy will have a similar appearance, characteristics, and temperament.

However, one of the main disadvantages of purebreds is that their bloodlines can run thin overtime, causing genetic defects.

Another disadvantage is the cost of purebred dogs. A purebred Poodle or Bichon Frise puppy can cost about $2,000. On the other hand, a Poochon puppy can cost from $600 to $1000, depending on the breeder.

One advantage to designer dogs is that breeders are able to eliminate certain traits which can make life difficult for the pet owner and for the purebred dog. Many smaller toy-breeds are prone to dental issues, epilepsy or hip dysplasia. The offspring of two different breeds rarely inherit these genetic defects since the bloodlines are not as close.

Another advantage to designer dogs is the breeder can fine tune the offspring's personality, traits and characteristics. For example, the Toy Poodle is renowned for being highly-intelligent but difficult to train. On the other hand, the Bichon Frise is adored by pet owners for its easy-going personality but tends to shed, making this breed a bad choice for allergy sufferers. But, when a Toy Poodle is crossed with a Bichon, the result is the popular Poochon – a low-shedding, easy-to-train dog who loves children and adults.

Even though the Poochon was bred for a specific personality, appearance and traits, a designer dog might appear or act more like one parent than the other.

History of the Poochon

The Poochon first appeared on the puppy scene in the early 1990's, in Melbourne, Australia. It is unknown who was the mastermind behind the cross of the Toy Poodle and the Bichon Frise.

The Poochon quickly gained popularity throughout Australia as an affectionate dog that could be trusted around small children. Within a few years, Poochons had charmed their way into the hearts and homes of pet owners around the world.

At the moment, Poochons are not a breed acknowledged by the American Kennel Club (AKC). However, they are recognized by the Designer Dogs Kennel Club and the International Designer Canine Registry. In the United States, many breeders have established clubs to promote proper breeding etiquette to ensure healthy, robust Poochon puppies.

First generation Poochons (Toy Poodle to Bichon Frise) rarely inherit genetic defects from their purebred parents. Second-generation (Poochon to Poochon) pups are more prone to inheriting genetic problems known to affect their grandparents – the Toy Poodle and Bichon Frise. For this reason, it is preferable to choose a first-generation Poochon.

As with most modern designer dog breeds, the exact history is unknown. However, taking a glimpse into the rich history of the Poochon's ancestors will give you an idea about his temperament, characteristics and appearance.

Toy Poodle

The Poodle's history dates back to more than 400 years ago. Even though the Poodle is considered to be the national dog for France, its origins began in Germany.

The word Poodle in the German language literally means "to splash in water." In France, the Poodle breed is called "Caniche," which means duck dog. Poodles were originally bred with a thick, curly coat to protect them as they retrieved birds from marshes for their masters. They are still used by a few waterfowl hunters today.

The Poodle's exaggerated show cut origins have nothing to do with fashion but function. Waterfowl hunters realized less hair would make the Poodle a more efficient and faster swimmer but at the same time, the dog would be more vulnerable to the cold water. As a compromise, Poodle owners left puffs of hair around their dogs' vital organs, upper torso, and joints to prevent the loss of too much body heat while wet.

Poodle

Poodles are considered to be one of the most intelligent canine breeds in the world. They are fast learners and thrive on learning new tasks. For centuries, they were prized as circus dogs for their ability to learn new tricks quickly and efficiently.

There are three variations of Poodles - Standard, Miniature and Toy. The Standard version is the oldest version of the Poodle. Toy Poodles, the Pochon's parent dog, were first bred in the early twentieth century as a companion dog for those living in small houses or apartments. In 1886, the Toy Poodle was recognized by the American Kennel Club as a breed. Ten years later, the Poodle Club of America was founded.

Toy Poodles are an extremely intelligent breed. They love learning and performing tricks and require mental and physical stimulation, such as going for walks with their loved ones or playing fetch in the park to burn off excess energy. They do not do well in environments where they are left alone for long periods at a time and tend to suffer from separation anxiety.

Toy Poodles grow to an average height of nine to eleven inches tall from the shoulder and typically weigh around six to nine pounds. Their dense and curly, non-shedding coat requires extra grooming to prevent it from becoming matted. The coat color comes in several shades such as apricot, black, blue, café au lait, brown, cream, grey and white. The average life expectancy for a Toy Poodle is fourteen to seventeen years.

Even though Toy Poodles are intelligent, they have a stubborn streak. But, once they are well-trained, they are some of the world's most loyal and affectionate dogs.

Toy Poodles are prone to maladies, such as dental problems, Addison's Disease, Hypothyroidism and progressive retinal atrophy.

Bichon Frise

Bichon Frise

The history of the Bichon Frise goes back to the early 1300's with origins from the Mediterranean region. The Bichon Frise was discovered by Italian sailors while visiting the Canary Island of Tenerife and soon after, became the preferred dog breed of Italian nobles and the upper class. During the 1500s, Italy was invaded a few times by France and these little beauties were among the spoils of war.

The Bichon Frise quickly gained popularity throughout France and Spain. It is most likely that this is where the Bichon Frise received its official name, which means "curly coat" in French. Throughout the following centuries, the Bichon Frise breed maintained its royal appeal with the upper class and royalty throughout Europe.

According to some historians, the Bichon Frise was bred for the sole purpose of sitting on the knee of the French King Louis XIV and, when we mention sit, we mean sit all day, every day. For this very reason, the Bichon Frise is prone to separation anxiety. The amount of separation anxiety that your Poochon has depends on how much of the Bichon genes he inherits. This type of dog easily adapts to new situations, as long as his human family is nearby.

In the early 1900s, French breeders standardized the breed, which was officially registered by the Société Centrale Canine of France in 1933.

In 1956, a French family moved to Michigan, USA with their Bichon Frises. Within four years, they were working with several different breeders within the United States. In 1964, The Bichon Frise Club of America was founded and in 1972, the American Kennel Club accepted the breed into its roster.

The Bichon Frise's appearance looks like a little, bundle of cotton or a real-life stuffed toy. Its charming, good looks and fluffy hair often gets them mistaken for a white Toy Poodle. It almost seems frightened by the sound of its own voice, unlike the Toy Poodle who loves to bark.

They do not like to be left alone for long periods of time, and they don't just love their families, they need to be with their families.

The Bichon Frise will grow to an average height of nine to twelve inches, from the shoulder and typically weigh around seven to twelve pounds. They have a soft, curly white coat with an occasional fleck of apricot or cream tones. Their coat doesn't tend to mat as easily as the Toy Poodle's tight curls. The average life expectancy for the Bichon Frise is fourteen to fifteen years.

Bichon Frises are prone to cataracts, Patellar Luxation and Urolithiasis and kidney stones.

Your Poochon can exhibit traits from both parents. For this reason, it is recommended that you carefully research breeders and determine whether or not the parent dogs have any health issues.

Physical Characteristics

Coat – The Poochon's coat is typically soft and curly, thanks to the Toy Poodle ancestry, which means that they will be light shedders and hypo-allergenic. Typically, the Poochon has a white coat, but other common colors are apricot, brown, grey or a blackish-blue tone. Since Poochons are non-shedders, they need to be brushed daily to keep them looking their best and to prevent any knots. Your dog will need to get a clipping every six to eight weeks to prevent matting.

Photo Courtesy of Claire Hughes

Eyes – The most common eye color for a Poochon is dark brown or black, but some can have light brown or amber colored eyes. Just a warning, don't be manipulated by your Poochon's big, warm, brown eyes. Behind them, is an intelligent pup who knows how to get what he wants from you.

Photo Courtesy of Hannah Inman

Nose – The Poochon's button nose is one of the breed's most endearing features. Often, they will have either a black or brown nose, which will get into plenty of trouble if you don't keep your garbage in a tightly closed bin.

Size – Poochons are considered to be a small dog with an average height of nine to fifteen inches at the shoulder, making them the perfect lapdog. Typically, a Poochon is considered to be full-grown at between twelve to eighteen months of age.

Weight – A full-grown Poochon can weigh between seven to sixteen pounds. Poochons are prone to weight gain, especially as they age. It is important to give them a healthy, wholesome diet and plenty of exercise as obesity can shorten the dog's lifespan and cause serious health problems.

Behavioral Characteristics

Poochons are rambunctious, affectionate and highly intelligent canines who are always looking for ways to please the family. They are considered to be fiercely loyal to their immediate families which can be a very endearing feature. However, this can lead to separation anxiety if your dog is left alone for long periods at a time.

Poochons can be a little boisterous at times, which is an inherited trait from their parents, the Toy Poodle and the Bichon Frise. Since the breed is prone to barking, they will need to be taught, while still puppies, to curb this tendency. Poochons are not good watchdogs, even though they might love the sound of their voice a little too much.

Your Poochon will make it his mission in life to befriend any other furry friends who live in the same household. However, a Poochon will also not hesitate to chase off any cats he may believe are trespassing on his property.

Don't be fooled by your dog's small stature. He is a fast learner and eager to please, which makes him quite easy to train.

One of the downsides to the Poochon's intelligence is that he will learn bad habits just as fast as good habits. This means that your dog will need to receive consistent obedience training as early as possible in life. Poochons respond favorably to all types of positive-reinforcement training methods, especially when there is a delicious treat involved. Later on, in this book we will discuss how to successfully use these methods in training your Poochon.

Your Poochon will test his boundaries and limits throughout his life. This is why training needs to be consistent and fair.

Photo Courtesy of
Caitlin Murphy

Is a Poochon the Right Fit for You?

Given their small stature and lovable personality, Poochoons are great dogs for any size of home. They don't need much space since they prefer to spend the majority of his time snuggled up on your lap. Poochons are an excellent dog for experienced and for first-time pet owners, as they are easy to train. But, as with most pets, they are best suited for families with certain characteristics.

Here are some general questions to ask yourself to see if you will make a good match for a Poochon:

- Can I give him at least thirty minutes or more of quality time daily for playing, socializing and exercising?
- Will I be able to spend less than five minutes a day brushing his coat and other grooming necessities, such as cleaning his teeth?
- Do I have time to take him for one or two short walks daily?
- Am I disciplined enough to train him to be obedient?
- Is there someone in the house most of the day to avoid him being left alone for extended periods?
- Can I reciprocate the unfailing love he will show to me day after day?

If you decide that a Poochon is the ideal choice for you and your family, you are not just getting a pet, you are gaining a new member of the family who will be dedicated to showing his new loved ones how much he adores them.

CHAPTER 2
Choosing a Poochon

It is easy to be won over by a Poochon puppy. His warm, dark eyes and floppy ears are practically begging you to bring him home.

Choosing the perfect Poochon may feel like an emotional roller-coaster ride, because you do not want to make the wrong choice. There are so many details involved in picking out your puppy. In this chapter, we will discuss everything you need to know about choosing your new best friend.

Photo Courtesy of Jo Shah

Buying vs. Adopting

Buy or adopt? Most people contemplating getting a dog will ask themselves this question at some point. Neither option is better than the other as there are pros and cons to both.

People can be passionate about both options, but ultimately, it is your decision and your decision alone. Nobody should pressure you to buy or adopt your new four-pawed companion. However, it is helpful to be well-informed about your options, so you can make the best choice for you and your family.

Adopting a Shelter Dog

There is quite a lot of negative stigma surrounding shelter dogs. One is that they will have behavioral issues or that they will be unpredictable. The facts show, though, that the majority of shelter dogs have been surrendered to the shelter because of a change of the pet owner's circumstances which have nothing to do with the pup's behavior.

- The majority of shelter dogs are already neutered/spayed and microchipped.
- You are saving the life of the Poochon that you are adopting and making space in the shelter for another dog in need.
- The shelter will be able to give you a general idea to the dog's personality, so there should be fewer surprises once you bring your Poochon home.
- Many adult Poochons are already potty-trained.
- The love and appreciation from a shelter dog is incomparable!

The costs of adopting can be considerably lower than buying a puppy from a reputable breeder. According to the Animal Humane Society, adoption fees for dogs and puppies can run from $120 to $670, depending on the shelter. On the other hand, buying a Poochon from a reputable breeder can cost anywhere from $700 upwards to $2,000. You can expect to pay even more if you buy a puppy with breeding rights.

- Since you are not raising your Poochon from puppyhood, you might not know his family history or where he came from.
- Many shelters have strict requirements for adopting one of their dogs to ensure the animal does not end up in a shelter again in the future.
- Since the Poochon is a relatively new designer breed in the United States, it can be difficult to find one in a local shelter.

- Finding a younger Poochon in a shelter can almost be impossible, and you may have to adopt an older pooch.
- Some dogs have been treated cruelly by their previous owners which has left them with emotional scars and behavior issues.

Photo Courtesy of Kellyann Soper

Shelters and Rescues

Animal shelters throughout the United States are overburdened with millions of abandoned pets each year. By adopting your Poochon, you are making room for other dogs. You are giving your dog a second chance to have a loving home plus, the cost of adoption goes directly towards the shelter, so that they can continue to help dogs in need.

Many Poochons are patiently waiting for someone to adopt them and take them to their new, forever home. The majority of these dogs are loyal, devoted, well-trained pets who just got the short end of the bone for one reason or another and have no place to go.

If you are ready to take the leap and adopt a Poochon, then you need to do some prep work before you stroll into your local shelter. You will need to ensure that your new pet will mesh with your lifestyle and family and, among other things, realize that there are hidden costs that come with adopting.

Although you may want to adopt your Poochon from a rescue, it can be difficult to know where to begin. Start by phoning local veterinarian clinics to ask for recommendations. They often know of dogs who might need re-homing or of reputable shelters in the area who might have a Poochon up for adoption. Another option is to do a Google search online for shelters or rescues in your country or state.

Sadly, some rescue shelters are just out to make money and flat-out lie to adopters, leaving them with aggressive, sick, pregnant or even dying dogs. Adopting your Poochon from an unethical shelter can quickly turn into a nightmare for you and your family. Here are some points to help make sure you find an ethical shelter.

The majority of shelters are honest and great to work with but here are some warning signs to watch for when adopting:

- The shelter refuses to let you meet your Poochon before adoption day. Most reputable shelters will let you meet with your dog as often as you like, even if you are still thinking it over. Just remember, though, someone else might adopt your Poochon while you are in the "thinking it over" stage.
- They refuse to take the adopted dog back. The majority of reputable shelters have a clause in the contract to allow you to return the dog within a specified time frame if something goes wrong. Hopefully, your Poochon will never have to return to the shelter.
- They adopt out Poochon puppies younger than eight weeks. By law, a shelter has to vaccinate and neuter/spay animals before putting them

up for adoption. Also, it is unethical and illegal to spay or neuter a puppy younger than eight weeks in many states.

- The shelter provides no or little proof of vaccinations. Avoid any shelter that is unwilling to provide proof of vaccinations.
- The shelter staff remind you of pushy used-car salesmen. A good shelter is more concerned about the dog's long-term care than making a sale. They will give you the time you need with the pooch to make your decision without pressure.

Many shelters provide free pamphlets or information sheets regarding the adoption process, requirements and, information on how to care for your Poochon. Each shelter or rescue organization has different requirements before starting the adoption process.

The following is a general guideline. The requirements might vary for each shelter:

- Most shelters will require you to show a government-issued photo ID proving you are twenty-one years or older.
- You will need to fill a straight-forward application form or an in-depth questionnaire.

Photo Courtesy of Jayne Dixon

- In some cases, you will need to provide references, such as permission from your landlord, verifying you are allowed to have pets.
- Some shelters or rescues will send a representative to your home to make sure it is safe and suitable for a dog.
- The shelter will observe how you and your family interact with the dog during a meet and greet before taking him home.
- Adoption fees will vary depending on the institution. Generally, the fee covers basic veterinary care, food, housing and care the dog received while in the shelter or foster care.

Once you start meeting different Poochons who are available for adoption, your emotions will be running in full gear. For this very reason, it is important that you do your research in advance. Be sure to read the adoption contract completely before signing and always ask the following questions:

1. Is the shelter responsible for any immediate health issues? Some shelters provide two-week health coverage in case health conditions unexpectedly pop up while other shelters expect the adopter to assume complete responsibility from day one.
2. Is your Poochon neutered or spayed? Many shelters automatically neuter or spay any dogs in their charge but others will charge extra for the surgery.
3. Can the shelter provide you with copies of your dog's medical records or background information?
4. What is the shelter's return policy? Many shelters have rules in case the adoption doesn't work out. Many shelters require the adopters return the dog to them, even if it is years later.

If you are still on the fence about whether you should adopt your Poochon, here are a few common myths about adopting a dog:

I don't know what I'm getting – Often shelters will be able to tell you, in detail about the Poochon's personality traits and behavior. The shelter will inform you about the dog's history as to why his former family surrendered him or whether he was a stray. Often, when shelter dogs are fostered, their foster parents will gladly share with you a wealth of information about your Poochon.

I cannot find a shelter that has Poochons – Since Poochons are a relatively newer designer breed it can be hard to locate a shelter with a dog that fits your criteria. Many shelters maintain a waiting list for specific breeds, so don't be shy to ask to be included on their list. Other excellent options are Petfinder.com and adopt-a-pet.com as they will help you find a Poochon in your locality that is up for adoption, simply enter your zip code and the type of dog you are seeking.

Shelter dogs have emotional baggage – Rescued dogs have a history, but their past may be a blessing in disguise as they will already be potty-trained and have a basic understanding of obedience training. All dogs, no matter their age, whether puppies or seniors, have a distinct personality. The shelter staff will help you find the ideal Poochon whose personality jibes with your lifestyle.

Shelter dogs were abandoned because they all have behavior issues - Quite often, dogs are given up because of an unexpected change of circumstances such as divorce, allergies, moving into housing that doesn't allow pets, financial issues or lack of time.

Buying from a Breeder

If you choose to buy a puppy, please do not support pet stores as they sell dogs from puppy mills. Later on, in this chapter we will learn about puppy mills and how to find a reputable breeder you can trust.

- You will be able to know where your pooch came from and how he was cared for and socialized up to the point you brought him home.
- Raising your Poochon from the time he is just a puppy will give you complete control in his training and upbringing.
- Breeders often will help you choose one of the puppies whose personality matches your lifestyle.
- Reputable breeders will provide you with everything you need to know about your Poochon, including family background, genetic testing, and the parent breed personality traits.
- Often you can pick the sex of the dog you prefer and the color of the dog's coat.

- Purchasing a Poochon from a reputable breeder is typically more costly than adopting.
- Often you will have to spend extra time researching to find a reputable breeder and might need to travel a considerable distance to pick up your puppy.
- Due to the Poochon's popularity, you might have to be placed on a waiting list for the next litter.
- Many responsible breeders will do a background check on the possible pet owner to ensure their pups are going to loving, caring homes.

As you can see, there are advantages and challenges to buying or adopting a puppy. Adopting a shelter dog is not for everyone and the same goes for raising a puppy. Whatever you decide, the advantages will outweigh the challenges once you start sharing your life with your loving, four-pawed best friend.

How to Find a Reputable Breeder

Finding a reputable breeder is the next important step in finding your Poochon. Breeders not only connect you with your perfect puppy, but you can rely on them throughout your Poochon's life. Breeders are often likened to your own private guide as they provide invaluable information from choosing the best puppy for you and how to care for it year after year.

When choosing where to purchase your Poochon, avoid pet stores or websites online, as the majority of these puppies come from puppy mills – inhumane, mass-breeding facilities.

Puppy mills are only concerned with churning out puppies for profit and completely ignore the needs of pups and their mothers. Often, puppy mills sell through social media, online classified advertisements, flea markets, and pet stores.

Mother dogs will spend their entire life in a cramped cage with little personal attention and, when they are unfit to breed, she will be dumped on the side of the road or killed. Due to a lack of sanitation and medical care, the majority of pups suffer from health issues and are prone to hereditary conditions, like respiratory disorders and heart diseases. There are more than ten thousand puppy mills in the United States alone and, they sell more than two-million puppies each year.

If you choose to adopt your Poochon, you may be wondering how the breed of a stray or surrendered dog is determined. Dogs at the Humane Society or local shelter are typically assessed based on appearance, which may not always be accurate. Alternatively, when a dog is surrendered to a shelter, the surrendering owner may provide breed information if they have it. At-home DNA testing is a relatively new concept and has gained popularity among dog owners who want to know a bit more about their dogs' genetic ancestry.

Here are some warning signs that indicate the breeder is really a puppy mill in action:

- The seller offers more than one type of purebred or designer dogs.
- They sell their puppies at less than eight weeks or younger.
- The breeder is located in another state but is willing to ship you the puppy without a face-to-face meeting first.
- The breeder refuses to show any potential clients where the puppies are bred and kept.
- The breeder doesn't ask any questions, and you can pay for the puppy without any previous screening.
- The seller makes no future commitment to you or the puppy. Reputable breeders always require you to sign a contract promising you will return the dog to them if you are unable to care for him in the future.

As with everything in life, it is important to do your research before signing a contract with the breeder. The best way to find a reputable Poochon breeder is asking for a referral from a local veterinarian, friends or shelters.

Here are a few tips to help you find a reputable breeder:

- **Meet the breeder** – The best way to get to know a breeder is by visiting their kennel or their home. If it is not possible to meet face-to-face, then organize a video-conferencing call to meet the breeder and their dogs. During the meet-and-greet session, observe the breeder and dogs. Does the breeder seem genuinely concerned about the well-being of their dogs? Are the dogs clean and well-fed? How do the dogs interact with the breeder and strangers?
- **Meet your Poochon's parents** – The best way to get a glimpse into how your puppy will be as an adult is to observe his parents. This will give you an excellent sense of your Poochon's personality traits, behavior, size and appearance.
- **Ask to see a FULL medical history** – Any trustworthy breeder will proudly show your Poochons parents' proof of health screenings. Also, the breeder will also inform you of any health conditions that typically affect Poochons and how to prevent them.
- **Be patient** – A reputable breeder often will have one or two litters a year, meaning you might have to wait a few months before you can actually welcome your little pup home. Normally, the breeder will not let you take your Poochon home until after three months, so it can mature and learn to socialize with his littermates.

- **Be prepared to fill out an application form** – Many reputable breeders will require any potential pet owners to fill out an extensive application form to allow them to see if you are good fit for one of their pups. This helps them ensure their dogs go to loving, forever homes.
- **Ask questions** – When you meet with the breeder for the first time, be prepared with a list of questions about your Poochon. Reputable breeders will happily answer all of your questions as they want to see their pups go to good, loving owners.

Important Questions to Ask the Breeder

Before you can bring your Poochon puppy home, you will need to do some casual detective work to assess the breeder. Buying a puppy is a big investment and commitment, so logically you want to make sure to get a healthy and happy Poochon from a breeder you can trust.

Photo Courtesy of Gillian Bull

Here are a few questions to ask the breeder:

Have the Poochon's parents been checked for any inherited genetic conditions?

Both of the Poochon's parents, the Toy Poodle and the Bichon Frise, are at risk for genetic health conditions, such as heart and hip problems. Make sure the breeder has tested and evaluated both parents and has the proper documentation to prove that neither parent has genetic diseases. Second and third-generation Poochons are more susceptible to inheriting genetic defects and diseases.

Can I meet the parents?

It might not always be possible to meet the father, but it is essential to see how the pup interacts with his mother and his littermates. Is the mother aggressive, shy or well-adjusted? Are the puppies hyperactive or docile? Observe the size of the parents and their temperament. This will give you a general idea what your puppy will be like.

How long have you been breeding Poochons?

You want to find out how much experience the breeder has had with crossing the Toy Poodle with the Bichon Frise. A reputable breeder should be knowledgeable about the Poochon's temperament, weaknesses and strengths.

Will my puppy be vaccinated and dewormed before coming home with me?

You want to make sure the puppies are being supervised by a professional veterinarian. Many reputable breeders will provide you with their veterinarian information so you can do a quick background check. Be sure to ask what shots your puppy will receive before you pick him up and when is he due for his next round.

How do you socialize the puppies?

Puppies learn proper social skills from their mother and littermates. Ideally, the breeder is raising the puppies in a family environment, where the pups are exposed to adults, children and a variety of noises.

Do you have any references?

Ask the breeder to send you a list of references. Call their clients and ask their opinions on the breeder, if they are happy with their Poochon and, if there were any problems how were they handled.

What is the parents' family history?

A passionate breeder will love to share the history of their dogs with anyone who will listen. Most likely, they will share the history of the purebred parents, the Toy Poodle and Bichon Frise, including registration details, which will allow you to check further into health tests and bloodlines.

How old is the mother and how many litters has she had?

Make sure that the mother was not mated before two years of age and she shouldn't be older than eight years old. During her lifetime, she should not have been bred more than four times, including this litter. If a C-section was required, she should not have had more than two in her lifetime.

Do you require a breeder's contract?

Most reputable breeders require a breeder's contract stating that you agree to not breed your Poochon and to have the dog neutered or spayed by a certain age.

Breeder Contracts and Guarantees

Often, we associate signing a contract when we are buying a house or leasing a car, not when we bring home a puppy!

Even though the idea of signing a contract can sound intimidating, for many breeders it is an opportunity to share their philosophies, advice and, expectations with the new pet owner. Breeders are taking a leap of faith to entrust their defenseless, beloved puppies to a stranger. By signing a contract, you are reminded of the enormous responsibility you are about to undertake.

Photo Courtesy of Paula Harrison

Although contracts can vary slightly, here are some of the basic elements you can expect to see:

- In the case the buyer is unable to care for their Poochon, then the family will return the dog to the breeder.
- If the dog is being used for breeding, then the contract will specify the terms. Often a dog used for breeding will have a considerably higher price.
- If the dog is not planned for breeding, then the contract will specify when the dog will have to be spayed or neutered.
- The buyer must follow the specified schedule of vaccinations.
- Some contracts guarantee against certain genetic health issues like hip dysplasia, only if the pet-owner takes certain precautions such as not letting their Poochon run up and down stairs for the pup's first twelve months.

If there is anything in the contract you have difficulty understanding or are unsure about, do not sign. Make sure you understand completely what you are signing beforehand. You can ask the breeder to send you a copy of the contract in advance, so you can read it carefully without feeling pressured.

Male vs. Female

Some people believe male dogs are more affectionate, while female dogs are easier to train and more protective of their families.

According to veterinarians and professional dog trainers, when it comes to dogs, there is no superior sex. The sex of the dog shouldn't have a major bearing on your decision. Instead, you should make sure that the dog's personality and energy level is a match for yours. Whether your Poochon is male or female, it's personality will be related to its surroundings and training.

It is worth mentioning that many of the biological differences between female and male dogs are related to their reproductive hormones and the dog's behavior is affected by hormones. Once the dog is neutered or spayed, the hormonal behavior will disappear overtime.

Even though both male and female dogs are excellent choices, there are a few physical, hormonal and behavior differences that you should be aware of:

Physical differences – Male dogs tend to be slightly larger in size when compared to their female littermates. Female dogs tend to mature faster than male dogs, making them easier to train.

Hormonal differences – Unneutered male dogs have a tendency to roam in search of a mate and to mark their territory by peeing on everything. Also, they will have an innate urge to mount anything that moves, even inanimate objects. Female dogs that have not been spayed will experience estrus (heat cycle) twice a year, producing a secretion to attract male dogs.

Behavioral differences – There are not many behavioral differences between female or male dogs. Your Poochon's behavior will be directly influenced by his training, upbringing and surroundings. However, studies show that dogs tend to get along better with the opposite sex. If you are bringing a second dog into your home, create the perfect balance with a female or male dog.

Instead of focusing on the sex of the Poochon, choose a puppy whose personality, behavior and demeanor will meld with your lifestyle.

Choosing the Perfect Poochon

Observing your Poochon interact with his mother and littermates can give you a glimpse into his temperament and personality.

Puppies raised in a family environment are often more socially adjusted to the typical commotion of an everyday household. Your Poochon should feel comfortable around strangers and not shy away from you. If the puppy seems anxious around the breeder or you, he most likely will grow up to be a nervous dog.

Avoid choosing the bold, pushy puppy, as he may grow up to be an aggressive dog who is difficult to train. Instead, befriend the quieter puppy who already has excellent manners. However, avoid puppies that tuck their tails under their legs or pull away from you when you try to pat them. Shy dogs often grow up into adult dogs who are easily frightened and may snap at younger children.

Watch how each puppy interacts with his littermates and when he is apart from them. Assessing the Poochon's reaction will give you a general idea how he will act in your house when he is temporarily left alone.

Give the puppy a quick health check by making sure he is in tip-top shape. Your Poochon's ears should be clean and odorless. The pup should be alert and aware of his surroundings. Even though it is typical for all dogs to have smelly breath, the pup's breath should not be offensive, and his curly coat should look soft, clean and shiny. There should be no signs of fleas or ringworm.

If the puppies do not look healthy, then the best choice would be to walk away. Even though the thought of leaving those adorable puppies behind will be difficult, it will save you from heart-break in the future.

CHAPTER 3

Preparing for Your Poochon

It is an exciting moment when you bring home your new Poochon! The first few months are most challenging but thoughtful pre-Poochon planning can help you to give your fuzzy bundle a head start to settle into his new family. Any of the initial bumps in the road will become happy memories that you will recall with a smile.

Photo Courtesy of Claire Hill

Puppy Proofing Your Home – Inside and Out

The big day has finally arrived!

Your curly Poochon is finally coming home. After months of searching for the ideal breeder or shelter, you finally found the perfect dog for you and your family. But before bringing your puppy home you need to puppy proof your home - inside and out.

Your Poochon will spend the majority of his time inside your house. It is extremely important that you take certain precautions and create a safe environment for him. You want to eliminate all dangers. All puppies are curious and, will investigate every nook and cranny of your house and backyard. No matter how intelligent your pooch is, he will love chewing on your furniture and your favorite pair of shoes.

Before you bring home your Poochon, get down on your knees and crawl from room to room, looking out for any possible hazards at a puppy's eye level. The Poochon's personality is often compared to Velcro. This means that where you are, the puppy will be right by your side. For this reason, be sure to pay extra attention to rooms where you will be spending the majority of your time.

In the kitchen

The kitchen is a fascinating place for your little bundle of fur. Your cabinets and drawers are ideal cubby holes to crawl into and explore. You can buy child-proof latches at the local hardware store which will help to prevent your curious pup from getting into trouble and, at the same time, keep him away from harmful cleaning supplies and foods. In chapter nine, you will find an extensive list of human foods that are considered toxic for all dogs.

If you have a garbage bin in the kitchen, make sure that it has a lid which tightly closes or, better yet, keep it tucked away under the sink with a childproof lock on the door. Poochons love to eat, so never under-estimate a Poochon left alone in the kitchen with food on the table. If possible, install a gate or door to keep your Poochon out of the kitchen, as necessary.

In the living areas

House plants are another hazard for your Poochon. Many plants are toxic if consumed by your little puppy. Place any house plants, on a table, counter or inside a spare room with the door shut. Here are some common house plants which are poisonous to dogs: aloe vera, ivy, orchids, Christmas cactus, lilies and jade plants.

Photo Courtesy of Melanie Panikker

If you have a fireplace, your Poochon can be harmed by flying ashes and flames. A simple solution is a protective fire screen. If you use fire-sticks to start your fire, be sure to place them up high and out of reach of your puppy.

Be vigilant in keeping living areas organized and tidy. Make sure that there are no small objects lying around such as shoes, cell phones or glasses – all of these items will tempt your curious and teething Poochon. Make sure that all blind cords and power cords are tucked away, out of sight or placed inside of chew-proof PVC tube.

In the office

Your office is full of everyday items that will make your Poochon feel like he is inside of a candy shop with so many temptations: papers, magazines, paperclips, staples, power cords, rubber bands, just to name a few. These items might be fun for your Poochon to play with but, if swallowed, they can cause serious issues, even fatal in some cases.

Be sure there is nothing up high that can fall on your Poochon if he accidently bumps into a piece of furniture. If your puppy accidently displaces a heavy vase, your dog may get seriously injured and damage your possessions.

In the bathroom

The bathroom can be a fascinating place for puppies. It contains all sorts of interesting places to squeeze in behind. However, if dental floss, medications, razors, cotton swabs, pills or soap are left within your Poochon's reach, they can easily be ingested. Expensive emergency visits to the veterinarian's office are quite common for puppies. Be sure to place all shampoos, conditioners, tissue paper, etc. inside of the bathroom cabinet or on a shelf out of his grasp.

Make sure the toilet seat is down at all times since, your curious Poochon could accidently jump into the toilet bowl and drown. Avoid automatic cleaning chemicals and keep the bathroom door closed. If you have a trash can inside the bathroom, make sure it has a locking lid or can be placed inside of the cabinet. Tuck away any dangling power cords and place childproof latches on the cabinets.

In the bedroom

Poochons are scent oriented and will gravitate towards anything that smells like you. If you don't want your clothing, socks or slippers to quickly become chewing toys for your puppy, then put them away. If you use mothballs, place them somewhere that your Poochon cannot reach. These are very toxic for dogs if swallowed.

Place any small objects inside the drawer or up high on a shelf. This includes items, such as jewelry, watches, hair clips and hair bands. Dirty, smelly clothes are especially tempting for your Poochon, so be sure to place them inside a laundry hamper. Poochons love to crawl and squeeze their way into small spaces. If you don't want him crawling under your bed, then make a temporary blockade with boxes.

In the garage or basement

The garage and basement have many objects that can be a health hazard for your Poochon. Place pesticides, rat and rodent poison, fertilizers, antifreeze, solvents, coolants, gasoline and oils inside a closed cabinet or on a high shelf. Make sure that any screws, bolts, nuts and nails are out of sight in a tightly closed jar or bag.

If you live in a colder climate, look for de-icing compounds that are safe to use around dogs, as many contain dangerous chemicals. Antifreeze has a sweet smell and taste that attracts dogs and can be fatal if ingested, even in small amounts.

In the laundry room

Your laundry is full of potential hazards; laundry detergents, cleansers, bleach, and fabric softeners can be dangerous for your Poochon if swallowed. While teething, puppies are tempted to chew and even swallow everything they can fit into their mouths, which can cause severe gastrointestinal issues.

Your washer and dryer can seem like a tempting place for your Poochon to crawl into for a little nap, so keep your appliance doors closed at all times. Do not leave buckets or bins waiting to be emptied anywhere near your pup. He could accidently fall in and drown.

The stairs

Most breeders will recommend that you avoid letting your Poochon walk up and down stairs at all costs, until he is at least twelve months of age. Poochons are prone to hip problems, as are the majority of smaller dogs. Using the stairs before their bones have fully matured can make any inherent problems worse. Also, smaller dogs can easily fall down the stairs, gravely injuring themselves. For these reasons, it is best to gate off the stairs until your Poochon is older.

In the yard

Your Poochon will love spending time outside with you and your family. If your yard is fenced, check to make sure that there are no holes that your pet can squeeze under and escape. If you have holes in your fence block them off with boards or chicken wire. Your Poochon can squeeze through a space much smaller than you would imagine. Be sure your fence is high enough so your Poochon cannot jump over it.

Walk through the grass in your bare feet looking for any objects that could potentially harm your puppy, removing any rocks, nuts or pinecones.

As noted earlier, certain plants can be poisonous to your dog or cause diarrhea and vomiting. This includes both common indoor plants and outdoor plants such as daffodils, foxglove, tulips, bird of paradise and lupines. Be sure to block off access to your plants while you puppy is roaming the yard. You can find a more extensive list of toxic plants for dogs on the Animal Poison Control website.

If you have a swimming pool, spa or ponds, be sure to block off access to them. Even though your Poochon can swim, he could still drown if he falls in and is unable to get out. Also, many of the chemicals used in maintaining swimming pools, spas and ponds are toxic. If your Poochon drinks the water, it could cause an upset tummy or diarrhea.

Poochons are considered to be hypoallergenic and are therefore low-shedding dogs. The American Kennel Club (AKC) asserts that there is no such thing as a 100-percent hypoallergenic dog, but hypoallergenic qualities include minimal shedding and a coat that doesn't produce much dander. Of the 19 breeds suggested by the AKC for allergy-sufferers, both the Poodle and Bichon Frise are listed.

Better safe than sorry

By taking the time to puppy proof your home before you bring your Poochon home, you are giving your dog a head start in settling into his new future home. As your Poochon settles in and gets older, he will learn basic obedience training and what is expected of him, so you won't need to be so vigilant with him.

Establish Puppy House Rules and Daily Routines

Before your Poochon first sets his paw into your house, you will need to establish certain house rules and your pup's daily routine. These steps will ensure your puppy will quickly adapt to his new life with less conflict.

Your Poochon might seem carefree and without a concern in the world, but his new routine will help him feel secure in his new environment. Remember, you have just taken your puppy away from the only world he has ever known, leaving his mother and littermates behind. Your dog just had a frightening car ride and has now arrived in a strange, new world with new smells, sounds and people.

Building a routine for your Poochon and establishing house rules will help your puppy understand what is exactly expected of him. Also, it will reduce any surprises that may cause any additional stress during the transition to his new family.

Have a family meeting

Before you bring your Poochon home, have a family meeting to decide who is going to be the primary puppy-parent. Below are a few topics to discuss with your family to make sure everyone is on the same page:

Where will he sleep? For small dogs, it is preferable to place his crate inside or near to someone's bedroom for the first year or at least until he is house-trained. In chapter six, you will find more information regarding crate training.

Is he allowed on the furniture? Your Poochon is a lapdog, so he will love spending hours each day cuddling with his family on the sofa. Will your dog be allowed on all the furniture or just the couch, but not the bed?

Where and who will be with him during the day? Poochons are very sociable pups and cannot handle being alone for long periods of time. If someone works from home, then place your pup's crate and playpen near the main workplace.

Are there any areas or rooms in the house that will be permanently off-limits? Too much freedom can be an overwhelming temptation for your Poochon. As your puppy grows to understand house rules, you can give him more freedom. Too much free roaming early on will lead to potty accidents, chewed up furniture and extra stress.

Where will his designated potty-area be? Whether you are training your Poochon to go to the bathroom inside or outside, each member of the family needs to know the procedure and where to take him.

How will you train him? Poochons respond favorably to positive training methods which will be discussed in chapter seven of this book. Choose the Poochon's main trainer and have the entire family reinforce the new behavior.

Establishing a routine and house rules are essential for your Poochon, even more so if there is more than one person living in the house. This will help maintain consistency. Your Poochon will be eager to adapt to his new family and to understand what is expected of him. The more consistent the entire household is at following rules, the sooner your dog will figure everything out.

Photo Courtesy of Sophie Clarke

Preparing Your Current Pets and Children

As the day draws closer to bringing home your little, bundle of fur, you will need to prepare your current pets and children for the arrival. First impressions have never been more important, so plan ahead for a smooth transition.

Before bringing home your Poochon, teach your children how to pick up the puppy and pat him. It is highly effective to use a stuffed toy in training your children how to do this. Explain to younger children that even though your Poochon looks like a stuffed bear, he isn't a toy. Even though they will want to play constantly with the new dog, tell them that he will need time to explore his new surroundings and rest.

Children tend to yell when they get excited, which can frighten the new puppy. Do practice sessions with your children, helping them to use softer, indoor voices, to avoid startling the Poochon.

If you have any pets who freely move about the house, be sure to ensure them of your love. Before leaving to pick up the new dog, take your pet(s) for a walk and give them a few yummy treats. Allow them to have access to all of the areas where they were previously allowed; otherwise, they will think you are punishing them. If you have a cat, ensure he will have access to high areas, so as to observe the new dog from a comfortable distance.

Create a new puppy sanctuary which includes a crate and an enclosed puppy pen. Allow the resident pets to explore the area freely before bringing home the new dog. If possible, ask the breeder to give you a piece of cloth that has the new puppy's scent. Let your present pets smell the scent as this will help them embrace your Poochon quicker.

Supplies

Before you bring home your new four-pawed best friend, there are several must-haves to have on hand. Once your puppy is home, you will not want to leave your adorable dog home alone to go shopping, so make sure you get these items beforehand. The following list is only a suggestion. You might discover you need to add more items later on.

Puppy toys – It is essential to give your puppy lots of different options for mental stimulation and teething. Chew toys basically teach your pooch to chew on certain objects instead of your furniture or shoes. Poochons especially love squeaky/crinkly toys and puzzle toys that contain a treat.

Crate – You need to find a suitable crate for your Poochon. There is no need to buy a puppy-sized crate then another crate when he is adult-sized.

Instead, save some money and time by getting a crate that is designed for your Poochon when he is full-grown. The crate should provide enough room for your Poochon to stand up, turn around and stretch. In chapter five of this book, we will discuss everything you need to know and more about crate training.

There are two basic types of crates - plastic and wire. Plastic crates are quite popular for bigger dogs and for travelling.

However, I personally prefer metal crates for the following reasons:

- Wire crates can easily be collapsed and can take up less space in storage. Plastic crates only come in two pieces and they take up more room.
- Some puppies can feel claustrophobic in a plastic pen, as there is less visibility. Wire crates provide a clearer view, allowing your pup to see everything around him. When he needs quiet time, you can easily place a blanket on top.
- The majority of wire crates come with a divider that allows you to adjust the size of the crate as your puppy grows.
- The plastic tray on the bottom of the crate makes for easy clean up as it simply slides up. Plastic crates will need to be taken apart to thoroughly disinfect them.

Clicker - A handheld device that makes a clicking noise, used in positive-reinforcement training. It is an essential training tool that you will start using from day one.

Poop bags - Being a responsible dog owner means picking up after your puppy. Look for poop baggies that are made from durable material and are easy to dispose of. It's even better if they are made from biodegradable materials.

Appropriate food - This includes whatever food your puppy has been eating (the breeder should give a few days' worth of the food they were feeding your Poochon) and what you have decided to feed your dog. To avoid stomach upset, make a gradual transition to the new food by mixing the two foods together.

Food and water dishes - Avoid brightly, colored plastic food and water dishes as the dyes can seep into your pup's food and water. Poochons tend to be sensitive to these harmful dyes which can cause eye irritation (teary eyes) and skin allergies. Instead, opt for stainless steel dishes that can be washed and disinfected in the dishwasher.

Pee pads (if you are pad training) - Pee pads are essential for indoor potty training, even if you are planning on training your Poochon to go outside. In the beginning, your puppy will have a hard time not urinating, so you can place the pee pad in an area close to his crate and slowly move towards the designated bathroom area.

Puppy bed or blanket – The crate will provide a sense of security for your pooch, but a soft warm blanket will make it feel like home. Look for

Photo Courtesy of Angela Marshall

an orthopedic mattress designed for the crate size and your pup's comfort. Also, your puppy will greatly appreciate having a soft, fluffy bed to relax on while watching television with his new family.

Toothpaste and toothbrush – You will need to get your Poochon used to having his teeth brushed from the very first week of bringing him home. Never use human toothpaste on your puppy. It contains an artificial sweetener called Xylitol, which is extremely toxic for dogs. Instead, look for toothpaste specifically designed for toy-sized dogs.

Training harness – A no-pull harness will protect your Poochon's tiny trachea. There is a reason why it is called a training harness because it teaches your pup not to pull while on his walk. Trust me – your Poochon will love his harness, just as much as you!

Leash and collar – Keep your Poochon safe and sound by having a durable collar and leash on, whenever you take him outside. I prefer a six-foot leash as it keeps my Poochon close to me but still gives him some freedom. The collar also is a place for your pup's identification tags, etc.

Stain and odor remover – Your Poochon will have a few accidents before he is trained. Look for stain and odor removers that destroys pet urine enzymes. These enzymes are like a red flag calling out for your dog to return to the exact same spot to urinate there.

Photo Courtesy of Ella Worley

Doggy treats – All dogs love treats, and your Poochon will not be the exception. Plus, treats are an essential part of training your Poochon. There is a wide selection of doggy treats available.

Nail trimmer – Look for a pair of nail trimmers that are designed for the toy-size breeds. They should be a good quality, as they need to last a long time. Check out the reviews online to make sure the trimmers are easy to use.

Hairbrush – The Poochon's fine and curly hair will need to be brushed daily to prevent it from becoming tangled and matted. The best brush for your Poochon is a small-sized comb and bristle brush, as it will quickly smooth out any knots. Also, stainless steel combs with round tips will brush your dog's hair without pulling or tugging.

Puppy gate and play pen – You are bringing home a new dog who doesn't have a clue about the boundaries and limits in your home. Placing him in a play pen or blocking access to stairs with a puppy gate will keep him safe, happy and properly contained.

Besides everything that you need to do to make your Poochon feel like a member of the family, do not forget to capture your memories together through your camera or phone. Also, the best thing you can give your curly bundle of fur is your unconditional love!

CHAPTER 4

Bringing Your Poochon Home

You are about to embark on a fun and occasionally crazy world of Poochon parenthood. For the next ten to fifteen years, you are going to receive more love and affection than you will know what to do with. This chapter will prepare for the first few days with your Poochon, so you and your dog can have great start to your new life together!

The Ride Home

For special occasions, it does not get much more exciting than bringing a puppy home for the first time. For you and your new best friend, this is a once-in-a-lifetime experience, so you want to make it memorable.

The first car ride home should not be taken lightly. It is an opportunity to get off on the right paw and start bonding together. Also, there are quite a few safety aspects to take into consideration, such as how to keep you and your dog safe on the journey home. Also, how should you prepare for the ride home and how often should you stop for bathroom breaks?

Before you head out to pick up your bundle of fur, make sure you are well-prepared by bringing along a blanket, a few chew toys, a leash and a collar, plus any cleaning supplies in case he has an accident in the car.

Upon arriving at the breeder's house to pick up your dog, any final paperwork will be dealt with outside before going inside to pick up your Poochon. The breeder probably will give you a small bag of the current dog food your puppy is eating to wean him onto the new food you are planning to feed him.

No food should be given to your pooch two to three hours prior to travelling to prevent car sickness. If the trip home is longer than three hours, be sure to bring along his food dish to give him a handful of food in case he gets hungry. Poochons love to eat and when they are hungry, they will clearly let you know by whining or barking.

Before hopping in the car and driving off with your new Poochon, take him for a short walk away from his mother and littermates so he can get used to being close to you. This will give your puppy an opportunity to relieve himself before getting into the car. Let your Poochon explore the car at his own pace by giving him a chance to smell his new blanket and

Photo Courtesy of Danielle Faulkner

crate. Leave the doors open and turn the car on so he won't be frightened from the engine noise.

But how should you transport your new dog home? Should he be placed inside a cardboard box on the floor or in a traveling crate? Or should he sit on your lap and be allowed to roam about the car freely? Is it better for him to sit in the back seat versus the front seat? Here are some common concerns:

Your safety – All puppies are curious by nature and if they are not secured inside of a crate, they can easily and dangerously become wedged under the pedals while you are driving.

Your Poochon's safety – Younger pups lack coordination and if allowed to wander around on the seats while the car is moving, they could possibly fall to the floor and hurt themselves. In addition, if you have to come to a sudden stop or swerve around a corner, your Poochon could be thrown off balance and be seriously injured.

Front or back seat? – In the United States, children who are seven years and younger are not permitted to sit in the front seat due to the impact of air bags. In the case of an accident, the air bag is instantly activated, releasing a punch that could seriously injure or kill a child. In the case of your itsy-bitsy Poochon, the force would, without a doubt, be fatal.

Crate or carried? – Many people, understandably, just want to cuddle with their adorable, little bundle of fur on the drive home. Some have a small cardboard box that they plan to place on the floor of the car, but this will not prevent a dog from climbing over the edges and gallivanting around your car. Your best choice is to use a crate.

You want your Poochon to associate good memories with his crate as you will be using it for training, so take the crate out of the car and place it on the ground with a few yummy snacks inside. Let your puppy go in on his own terms, so he feels safe. Place a soft blanket and chew toy inside.

When choosing a travel carrier consider the following points:

- **Find the correct size** - A twelve-week-old Poochon weighs approximately one to two pounds and should be slightly smaller than a soccer ball. A full grown Poochon will weigh between seven to seventeen pounds and range from nine to fifteen inches in height. The carrier or crate should be big enough for your pup to stand up in and to turn around.
- **Design matters** – Look for a dog carrier that has passed third-party crash tests and comes highly reviewed. A poorly designed dog carrier can be hazardous in an accident.

Photo Courtesy of
Adele Hughes

- **Choose a style** – There are two basic styles of travel carriers for dogs – hard and soft cover. Hard covers offer superior protection for your dog and are preferable if traveling long distances. Soft covers offer less protection for your dog but are easier to carry than the heavy, cumbersome hard-covered carriers.

Bathroom breaks – Puppies haven't learned to control their bathroom urges, so if the drive home is longer than two hours, you may have to make a bathroom stop. Avoid spots that are frequently visited by other dogs. This is because your Poochon puppy hasn't received all of his vaccinations yet and you do not want to risk him picking up a contagion.

Even if your puppy doesn't go to the bathroom, it gives him a good opportunity to stretch his legs. Be sure to put the leash and collar on your Poochon before you let him out of the car, for any rest stops. This will help prevent him escaping and running onto the road and getting hit by a car.

Two is better than one – Ask a friend or family member to go with you to pick up your Poochon, as they can drive the car while you sit in the back seat next to your puppy. Poochons tend to bond quickly to people they encounter early on. Plus, remember this is the first time he has been for a car ride and separated from his family, so being alone can be a terrifying experience.

Car sickness – Many puppies and older dogs suffer from car sickness. Watch for your dog pointing his nose towards the floor, lips wrinkled up, drooling and heaving. Lay a towel under him to facilitate cleanup. Cover his crate with a blanket to help him feel more secure or open the window a crack to let in fresh air.

Climatic considerations – Puppies have a difficult time regulating their body temperature and are prone to hypothermia and hyperthermia. Make sure the inside temperature of your car is comfortable and never leave your dog alone in the car.

Psychological well-being – Come straight home. This is not a time to stop and grab some groceries or stop off for a quick visit with friends. Keep the entire trip quick, smooth and simple. Remember that your pup is already having an incredibly stressful day.

Make it a positive experience and avoid creating emotional scars that could resurface later on in his life, such as separation anxiety. Talk to your Poochon in a soft, calming voice to make him feel safe and sound. If you play music in the car, choose relaxing tones that transmit tranquility.

The First Day

Bringing a new dog home is a joyous occasion. You have been waiting for this moment, perhaps for months. However, even though you are bursting with excitement about starting your new life with your puppy, remember that he is overwhelmed and exhausted. After all, he is in a strange place, with new scents and people he doesn't know. Here is everything you need to know about making your Poochon's first day easier.

Your Poochon is still a baby. Up until today, he has spent his entire life near his mother and littermates. All the sights, noises and smells that once comforted him are gone and replaced with strange new ones. To help your

Photo Courtesy of Paula Harrison

puppy settle into his new home quicker, ask the breeder to give you a piece of bedding or a snuggle toy that smells like his mother and littermates.

Keep your Poochon's home coming low-key and stress-free. Be sure to phone your friends and family ahead of time to let them know you will not be having a meet-and-greet the first day your pup comes home. The fewer new people your dog has to meet on his first day, the better.

A dog from a shelter might arrive sleep deprived or stressed, so don't be surprised if the first thing he does after exploring his surroundings is to fall into a deep slumber. Your adopted Poochon will need a short period of time to adjust to his new routine and structure, no matter if he was in the shelter for a few days or a couple of months. He will need to learn new habits and rules as he settles into his new, forever home.

There is no need to hurry and introduce your new dog to your other pets. You will have plenty of opportunities to teach them how to get along and slower introductions will allow them to get acquainted with each other on their own terms.

Let your Poochon explore his new surroundings little by little; he will want to smell everything and everyone.

One of the first things you need to show your Poochon is where his designated potty area is and his water and food dishes. This is an excellent time to start teaching your dog his new name. Within a few days, he should know it like the back of his paw. Show him where his home base will be and throw some yummy snacks onto his bed, so he enters the crate on his own accord.

Resist the urge to shower him with attention. Instead, let your Poochon dictate the pace of his interactions. Some puppies are out-going and enthusiastic; others might be standoffish and prefer to sit back and drink in their new surroundings. Avoid chasing your Poochon around the house or cuddling him, even though he wants to play or be snuggled. Teach him to trust you by sitting on the ground and let your dog come and go as he wishes.

If you have younger children, be sure to clearly explain to them beforehand how to handle a baby puppy. Never let your children play with the Poochon unsupervised, as their excitement can startle the little puppy.

If you normally work on the day you plan to bring your Poochon home, make sure you request time off, so you can spend as much time with the puppy as possible. After all, it is the first day that you embark on an incredibly special friendship!

Photo Courtesy of Barbara Trister

The First Night Home

For the first few nights, even weeks, you are going to be sleep deprived. Puppies tend to sleep between sixteen to twenty hours a day, but they have near-hourly bathroom needs. When your Poochon wakes up, he will start whining or crying to let you know that he has to go to the bathroom. You will not have much time to get him to his designated potty spot. So, have a spot close by and run!

Place your Poochon's crate in the area where you want him to sleep. Some new puppy owners prefer to put the crate inside their bedroom so they can hear when their puppy wakes up. Once you pick a sleeping place for your puppy, don't change it until he is potty trained.

Scent is one of your Poochon's strongest senses. On his first night, sleeping without his littermates, he will feel overwhelmed. If the breeder gave you

Photo Courtesy of Jade Panton

a small piece of mama-scented towel or blanket, place it inside of the crate to soothe your anxious little puppy.

Looking for a few other tricks to calm your new friend to sleep on his first night away from his mother?

Try hiding an old-fashioned alarm clock under his bedding. The steady tick-tock sound resembles the sound of his mama's heartbeat. Or try placing a hot water bottle under his blanket to keep him toasty warm at night.

From the very first night, you need to start teaching your Poochon bedtime is sleepy time and not playtime. If he barks to go to the bathroom, take him to the designated bathroom area. Once he goes to the bathroom, reward him with a treat, then take him back to his crate to go back to sleep.

Do not be fooled by those big brown eyes! He needs to learn nighttime is for sleeping, not for playing.

Your new pup's bladder has not built up enough control to get through the entire night without needing to go to the bathroom. It will take a number of weeks before you will be able to sleep through the night without having to rush him to his bathroom spot. Expect to get up at least five to six times, the first few nights, to take him to the bathroom.

Choosing a Reputable Vet

Choosing the right veterinarian for you and your Poochon is something that you should not take lightly. The veterinarian you choose could potentially save your dog's life and is responsible for keeping him healthy. Plus, the veterinarian you choose will play a significant role in your Poochon's life, so take your time searching for the right one. Here are some things to consider before you choose a veterinarian.

Word of mouth – Asking for personal recommendations is one of the best ways to discover a reputable veterinarian. Be sure to consult with friends, family and colleagues with pets, for advice and opinions on veterinarians in your locality.

Find a veterinarian who specializes in treating dogs – Not all veterinarians are created equal, especially if you live in a rural setting. Often, veterinarians have more experience with treating horses, cows, etc. than canines. You definitely want a veterinarian who is experienced in treating dogs. Be sure to ask the veterinarian clinic how much experience he has treating small dogs like the Poochon.

Make sure they are a licensed veterinarian – Most of us just assume that all veterinarians are licensed professionals, but that is not always the case. Make sure the vet is licensed in your state as a veterinarian and not just as a registered veterinary technician. On the American Animal Hospital Association (AAHA) website, you will find a list of accredited and licensed veterinarians in your locality, as well as an evaluation of the facility, staff, patient care and equipment.

Consider the cost and the location – If an emergency occurs, will you be able to get to the vet's office quickly? Choose a veterinarian whose office is less than one hour drive from your house and ask if they do house calls to your area. Costs can vary from vet to vet, so be sure to inquire about their prices to make sure they are a good fit for your budget.

Do both you and your Poochon feel comfortable? – You need to feel comfortable around your vet as you need to be able to tell him everything about your Poochon. The staff should be friendly and generally seem to love animals. The same goes for your dog; he needs to feel at ease around the vet. If you sense that your Poochon seems distressed, fearful and aggressive around the vet, that is a red flag to move on.

Look for a clean facility – Ask to have a look around the office to check out the level of cleanliness. If the place seems dirty, dingy or foul-smelling, then that is another sign to move on. A veterinarian's office is a medical facility, so it should be just as clean as a hospital or clinic for humans.

If you have any problems with the vet you choose, do not hesitate to switch facilities. Veterinary clinics expect clients to come and go. However, before you depart, be sure to request a complete copy of your Poochon's medical file. You can ask that your dog's health records be faxed or mailed to either you or your new vet.

Your Poochon's First Vet Visit

Once you have found a veterinarian who you feel comfortable working with, book an appointment for a meet-and-greet for your Poochon before his actual visit for his vaccines. Any reputable veterinarian will be extremely busy and will not have time for drop-ins unless it is an emergency. Therefore, make an appointment and arrive early, so your Poochon can get used to the scents, noises and surroundings.

This will allow your puppy to associate positive memories with the veterinarian's office. The employees may slip your Poochon a treat or two. Many pet owners who skip this step end up with dogs who are absolutely petrified of going to the vet's office.

When you go in for your Poochon's actual first real vet's visit, be sure to take along with you any paperwork regarding your dog, such as his vaccination and health records from the breeder or shelter. Most likely, this paperwork will stay with the veterinarian's office in your Poochon's personal file at the veterinarian office. If you want copies for yourself, make photocopies before going to the vet's office.

What should you expect during the first vet's visit?

You will be allowed into the examination room with your Poochon. Be sure to bring along some of his favorite treats. Be calm and relaxed, while talking to your pooch use an upbeat, happy voice, praising his good behavior.

The veterinarian will weigh your Poochon, check his temperature through his rectum, examine his eyes, ears, mouth, paws, teeth, genital region and fur. Then the vet will listen to your dog's heartbeat and lungs using a stethoscope. The veterinarian will palpate your dog's lymph nodes and abdominal areas. Once the general exam is finished, the vet will administer swiftly any vaccinations and dewormers required.

The vet will most likely discuss any future medical procedures your Poochon might need, such as spaying or neutering and microchipping. If you have any questions regarding your pup's general health, now would be a good time to ask. Your veterinarian will give you a vaccine schedule for your Poochon. Be sure to place future dates on your calendar so you don't forget.

CHAPTER 5

Laying a Solid Foundation to Train Your Poochon

Children need to learn the alphabet before learning to read, as it will become a foundation that will set them up for success throughout their lives. Similarly, your Poochon will need to learn the A-B-Cs of basic training and boundaries, as it will become the foundation upon which all future training will be built.

Your primary job is to introduce your little puppy to his new world in a positive way. In this chapter, we will discuss how to avoid common training mistakes and how to nip bad behavior in the bud.

Photo Courtesy of Leanne Patel

Disobedient or Bad Parenting?

There is an old English saying – "To err is human," which means we all make mistakes whether we want to, or not. That saying could not be truer than when it comes to puppy training. Often, these training errors are not life-threatening, and they can be amended. But they definitely will slow down the entire training process, causing irritation on both ends of the leash.

Here are some of the most common mistakes people make while training their puppy. This is to help you avoid making them:

Waiting too long to start training - Training your Poochon should begin the minute he comes home with you regardless if he is a puppy or an older dog from a shelter. Avoid the temptation to wait until he outgrows his puppy stage, as he will develop bad behavior and habits in the interim.

Younger Poochons might not be able to learn advanced commands due to a lack of agility. They will, however, be able to start learning potty training and basic commands like "come" and "stay."

Too lengthy training sessions – Longer training sessions are impractical for many reasons. Puppies and adolescent dogs have a short attention span. They tend to become bored or distracted quickly. Instead of one long training session each day, break the classes up throughout the day to keep your pooch interested in learning. Keep training sessions short and sweet – aim for five to ten minutes each session.

Not enough practice – There is an old Russian proverb – "Repetition is the mother of learning," which means repetition is the key element in learning. Through repetition, a skill is practiced and rehearsed until it becomes easier. Remember when it comes to your Poochon, practice makes perfect!

Many dog owners make the big mistake of assuming their dog has learned everything in his obedience classes. But fast forward a few weeks, even a few months and the dog has forgotten everything he has learned. What happened? Dogs, just like us, get rusty. Be sure to reinforce your dog's skills daily; all you need is a few minutes each day.

Rewarding negative behavior – Many dog owners do not realize they are rewarding their pup's bad behavior. For example, they might comfort their puppy because he was frightened from being left alone for a few minutes or by letting their puppy bark at the neighborhood cat, because it is cute. This leads to repetition of the same unwanted behavior.

Poochons are very sociable dogs who thrive on their owner's attention. Whenever you give your pup attention, he understands that you are pleased with his current behavior and it should continue. If your dog's behavior is undesirable, like jumping up, barking, whining or begging, then the best thing you can do is to completely ignore your dog until the behavior stops.

Inconsistency – Inconsistent training will confuse your Poochon. For example, let's say your pooch is not allowed on the couch. But occasionally you make the exception for your dog to come cuddle with you on the couch. But then you turn around and discipline your pup for sitting on the couch. He will not understand what he did wrong, as one minute he is allowed on the couch and the next, he is not.

Photo Courtesy of Geraldine McGrath

Strive to be constantly consistent with your Poochon. For example, every time you come home do not give your fuzzy ball of fur any attention until he is sitting on the floor and not jumping up. This can be difficult, especially when you have had a bad day at work. Consistency will prevent your Poochon from becoming confused and in the long run, will make the training process easier for the both of you.

Impatient – Training your Poochon takes time and you need to remember that every dog learns at a different pace. Avoid getting frustrated while training your dog, as he will pick up on your negative vibes. Training sessions should be upbeat and positive, so make sure your attitude is in the right frame of mind first.

If your Poochon is struggling to learn something, instead of becoming frustrated with him: stop and consider whether this is a good time or has the session gone on for too long? Remember, training sessions should be short and sweet (about five to ten minutes) and end on a positive note. If you are impatient and getting irritated with your pup, stop the training session by doing an easy action that your puppy already knows such as "sit" and end with a reward.

Just a word of caution: never, ever train your Poochon when you are in a bad mood. This is a recipe for disaster. You could easily take your frustration and anger out on your poor, defenseless dog if he makes a mistake. Instead, make a cup of tea and snuggle up with your Poochon on the couch until your mood improves.

Lack of daily routine – Poochon's love routine. During the first few months with your dog, he will learn where to eat, play, sleep and go potty. By establishing a specific routine and time schedule when these things happen, you will promote proper behavior and confidence for your dog. Poochons are eager to please their new family, so use this to your advantage!

An inconsistent routine can lead to potty accidents and an increase in undesirable behaviors, such as barking or biting. Be sure to establish a manageable routine for your Poochon before you bring him home. This will help to avoid unnecessary stress and get your pup on the right track as soon as possible.

Harsh discipline – Studies have proven that using harsh discipline in dog training is counterproductive. In general, Poochons respond better to training when combined with positive reinforcement, like praise and treats. Harsh discipline involves yelling, hitting, use of physical-force, leash-jerking, grabbing at the scruff of the neck and staring down. All of these negative actions will seriously affect your dog in the following ways:

- They may cause your Poochon to become aggressive, even violent around strangers, putting you and others in danger.
- They may cause your Poochon to become fearful and suffer from separation anxiety later on in life.
- These methods teach your dog to distrust humans.

When you hit or yell at your dog, you are teaching him to fear you, you break his trust and weaken his confidence. There is no place for any type of harsh discipline in training your dog.

How to Train an Older Shelter Dog

If you have adopted an older dog from the shelter, congratulations! Shelter dogs make excellent family pets. No matter, why your Poochon ended up in the shelter, with a little tender, loving care, he can become a happy, well-adjusted member of your family.

Most likely your adopted Poochon already has received some obedience training, and just needs a little refresher course. Or perhaps, his past has triggered some behavioral issues. That is why your older Poochon will need a little extra time and patience to learn his new boundaries and what is expected of him.

HELPFUL TIP
Separation Anxiety – Practice Makes Perfect

Poochons are such small, delightful dogs that you may be tempted to take yours everywhere you go! But it's important to give your dog practice with being alone so that when you inevitably need to leave, your dog won't suffer from separation anxiety. A crate can be a useful tool for practicing this behavior. Try leaving your dog in the crate for short periods while you are in another room, and slowly increase the length of time over subsequent sessions. Your dog will eventually build up the confidence to spend time alone when you need to be elsewhere.

Adjustment period - As you know, adopting a dog means it comes with a history. The stress of being abandoned at the shelter and away from his previous family can make your pooch wary of his new surroundings. Be sure to give your Poochon time to adjust to his new home, family and other pets. Your Poochon may need only a few hours to get used to his new place or a few weeks. During the adjustment period, be sure to follow a regular routine to keep things predictable and consistent.

Establish boundaries - Training begins from the very first minute you bring your Poochon home. Avoid the temptation to pamper your pooch the

Photo Courtesy of
Jen Swanson

first week or two to make up for the time spent in the sterile, cold shelter. Older Poochons are wise beyond years and they know how to use those big, dark eyes to get away with bad behavior.

Be aware, if you let your Poochon get away with unacceptable behaviors when he first comes home, then it will be much harder to train him to stop doing it later. For example, this could be chewing on the furniture, relieving himself on the carpet or climbing up on the furniture. Be sure to establish your Poochon's boundaries from day one and make sure the entire family is aware of them and enforces them.

Be patient - Your Poochon's life experiences can make him nervous about his new surroundings. Be patient and give him time to adjust. Once your Poochon realizes he has found his forever home, he will quickly settle in.

If you need to correct your Poochon's bad behavior, redirect his attention to a more appropriate behavior. For example, if your Poochon tends to chew on the furniture, then give him a chew toy. Once he starts chewing on the toy instead of the furniture, praise him and reward him with a treat. It might take a few weeks or months to erase years of bad habits, but with patience, he will improve.

Stick to a schedule - Shelter dogs need a routine. Your adopted Poochon has spent the last couple of days or weeks in an unpredictable and stressful kennel area. By establishing a schedule for feeding, walking, training sessions, playtime, and bedtime you are giving your Poochon peace of mind and stability.

Challenges when Teaching Older Dogs

The saying, *"you can't teach an old dog new tricks"* has been around for decades. The truth is, you can teach an old dog new tricks, and it is not that much different from teaching a puppy.

Actually, there are quite a few advantages to teaching older dogs, compared to puppies, due to their longer attention span. However, your older Poochon might need a little extra motivation than a puppy, especially if his previous owners mistreated him.Even though your Poochon might not be as agile or mentally sharp as a puppy, he still has a built-in desire to please you.

One of the most common mistakes that pet owners make while training a shelter dog is assuming that they have the stamina of a puppy. Older Poochons get tired faster than a younger dog, perhaps because of health problems.

Here are some suggestions to consider when training an older dog:

- Keep training sessions upbeat and positive. If you or your Poochon become agitated, anxious or nervous, then it is best to take a break.
- Old joints do not like doing the same movement over and over again. Avoid asking your Poochon to "sit" twenty times in a row without taking a break. Doing so may cause your pooch pain and may make him slow to respond.
- Keep training sessions short and sweet.
- Recognize and take into consideration your Poochon's limitations.
- Use verbal and hand signals. Older dogs may be hard of hearing so the hand signals will help.
- Positive reinforcement is your secret weapon, especially treats. If you are worried about weight gain, chop unsalted, boiled, skinless chicken breast into small pieces.
- Be aware of the temperature. Older dogs are more sensitive to heat and cold than younger dogs.
- Train on soft surfaces. Choose soft surfaces such as carpet, grass or a yoga mat to make training sessions more comfortable for your elderly Poochon.
- Practice one trick at a time, as multiple tricks may be confusing and frustrating for your elderly dog.

Remember that training sessions should be fun and give you moments to bond with your Poochon. If your dog's health and age prevent him from learning a new trick, concentrate on making him feel comfortable, loved and cared for.

Obedience Classes

Whether you have a puppy or a shelter dog, obedience classes can help your Poochon learn to behave correctly at home or while out and about. Typically, obedience classes teach the pet owner how to teach their dog basic commands, such as lie down and sit. Also, your Poochon will learn socialization skills required to interact with different people and other dogs.

Before your Poochon begins any type of obedience or socialization classes, be sure your dog has received all of his vaccinations at least seven days prior.

Beginner obedience classes for dogs often will be divided into age groups and will teach your Poochon the following:

- Basic commands, such as sit, lie down, come and roll over

- Not to pull on the leash while going for a walk
- Not to jump up on other people or dogs
- Not to chew on your furniture
- Socializing with new people, dogs and places

Obedience classes are designed to teach basic training. So do not expect them to resolve any major issues such as aggression, separation anxiety, depression and excessive barking.

Photo Courtesy of Claire Hughes

The majority of obedience classes will meet for approximately one hour each week for a period of eight to ten weeks, depending on the program. The success of each course will depend entirely on the pet owner having daily training sessions with their dog, putting into practice what they learn each week. Here are some suggestions to consider when choosing the right obedience course for your Poochon.

Ask for referrals – The best place to start is by asking fellow dog-lovers, friends and family, and of course, your veterinarian for recommendations on obedience classes in your locality. In addition, you can also look online for reviews on the obedience course you are interested in.

Check their credentials – Look for an instructor who has credentials from one or more of the following associations: National Association of Dog Obedience, Association of Pet Dog Trainers, National K-9 Dog Trainers Association, and the International Association of Canine Professionals.

Visit a free class – Most obedience classes will let you observe a class or two before signing up for the entire course. If they do not allow you to sit in on a class for free, even without your dog, then that is a warning sign to look for another course. Transparency is essential for the well-being of you and your dog. Be patient in searching for the best choice for you and your Poochon.

Watch out for red flags – Obedience classes are not only about teaching your Poochon new commands, but also about socializing your dog with other people and dogs. The class should also be fun and enjoyable for your dog. Never accept an instructor who encourages pet owners to yell or hit their dogs or use potentially harmful techniques or devices. Dogs are very intuitive. If you notice your Poochon is uncomfortable around the instructor, there probably is a good reason.

Pick the right fit – The best dog obedience course should be a good fit for your budget, driving distance, quality and content, and of course your overall first impression of the instructor. Be sure to take into consideration any referrals you received to help choose the best obedience course for you and your Poochon.

When to get professional help

It can be a challenge to figure out if your Poochon is simply misbehaving or if he has behaviorial issues. If your Poochon does have a behavioral problem, normal training tactics may not be enough. There are a few extreme cases where you might need help:

Biting – It is normal for a puppy to go through a biting stage while he is teething. However, when a dog viciously bites and snaps, that is unacceptable. Aggressive behavior cannot be fixed by common obedience classes. In this case, the dog will need professional help by a dog trainer who specializes in behavioral issues.

Separation anxiety – Poochons often suffer from separation anxiety but the problem can often be directed by working one-on-one with your pooch. But if you have tried and tried to reprogram your Poochon's bad behavior and he still goes into a destructive panic mode every time you leave the house, then he may need specialized training and medication.

If you need professional help for your Poochon, the best place to turn to is your vet for recommendations.

Unacceptable Behavior from Day One

Many dog behaviors that we consider to be inappropriate are actually an instinctive part of their canine personality, such as digging, barking or rolling on a dead animal. For your pooch, these activities are innate behaviors, but you can train your Poochon to at least minimize these habits.

Here are some helpful strategies to nip bad behavior in the bud:

- **Burn off excess energy** – A tired dog is a well-behaved dog. If your Poochon is not getting adequate exercise, he will channel his energy into another activity like chewing your furniture or digging up your flower garden.
- **Prevent bad habits from developing** – Keep any objects such as toys and shoes out of sight, houseplants off the floor, electronical cords tucked away, etc. It is easier to prevent bad habits from happening if there are no temptations in the first place.
- **Reward desired behaviors** – Anytime you notice your Poochon is behaving correctly, be sure to bend down and pat his hand and tell him what a good boy he is. For example, he is walking beside you, on the leash without pulling, or he is sitting quietly, waiting to greet you, instead of jumping.
- **Be consistent** – If you do not slip your Poochon a piece of turkey from the kitchen table but your husband does, the dog will learn to beg. Or you make him sit on the floor by the couch, but your children let your dog hop up on the couch, guess what he will do? Everyone needs to be consistent in following the same rules.

Chewing

Dogs naturally chew on objects for a number of reasons. In the case of puppies, chewing is a way to relieve pain caused by teething, and for older dogs, they chew on bones to keep their jaw strong and teeth clean. However, this behavior can quickly turn into a habit if they are not taught what objects are appropriate for chewing and what is not.

If you catch your Poochon chewing the wrong thing, instead of scolding him, quickly distract him by clapping your hands. Then replace the object with a chew toy. Never use old shoes or socks as chew toys.

Barking

Your Poochon may vocalize in one way or another, by barking, howling, whining or more. Barking is considered normal behavior for dogs unless it is excessive. Your Poochon might be barking out of excitement, boredom, or fright or to alert you that something is out of the ordinary.

If your Poochon is barking for your attention, simply ignore him until he stops barking then praise him for being quiet. Do not even look or speak to your Poochon while he is barking, as he will think you are encouraging him to bark even more. If your pooch is barking at a stranger, such as the pizza delivery guy, tell him it is okay and introduce him to the new person, reassuring him there is no reason to be scared.

Mounting

Mounting and humping are normal behaviors for both male and female dogs. Your Poochon may attempt to mount moving and inert objects, such as people, other animals, dog beds and toys, or he will just lick himself. Neutered and spayed dogs may continue mounting or humping because this behavior feels good.

If you notice that your Poochon is trying to mount or hump, quickly try to distract him. Play a game, toss him a chew toy or ask him to perform a trick such as give a paw. Over time, your dog will forget about this behavior, but only if you nip it in time.

Digging

If given the chance, all dogs will love to dig up your flower garden. It is just part of their natural instinct. Your Poochon is prone to digging because of his parents' hunting heritage. Dogs generally dig to burn off excess energy or due to boredom, hunting instinct, a desire to conceal a bone or toy, to cool off or to escape.

Try to determine the reason why your Poochon is digging up your backyard, then work to eliminate the cause. For example, if your dog is digging out of boredom, then spend more time with him exercising each day. If your pup is digging for no apparent reason, dedicate a small part of the garden or sand box where he can freely dig. Teach your Poochon that it is only acceptable to dig in a certain spot.

Separation Anxiety

Separation anxiety is one of the most common behavioral issues with Poochons and it occurs when your dog is left alone for a short period of time or for a few hours. Your Poochon can exhibit one or all of the following destructive behaviors: excessive, barking, whining, chewing, inappropriate urination and defecation. Often a dog suffering from separation anxiety will follow his owner around constantly.

Separation anxiety is one of the most difficult habits to break and often needs dedicated training with professional help. Here are simple steps to prevent separation anxiety from developing in the first place:

- Ask a family member to hide near your Poochon's crate, but out of sight.
- Place your Poochon inside his crate with a chew toy and few treats. Avoid making a big show about leaving.
- Ask the family member who is hiding, before entering the house, how your pup behaved via text message. If he behaved, calmly greet him and reward his good behavior.
- Each time that you leave, slowly increase the time away, until your Poochon learns how he is supposed to act when he is left home alone.

Running away

Your Poochon's hereditary genes are programed to sniff out a small animal or rodent, so his little nose is going to get him in trouble!

If you have a fenced-in back yard, get down on your knees to make sure there are no small holes or spaces that your Poochon can squeeze under and escape. If you don't have a fenced in backyard then keep him tied up when left outside unsupervised.

Jumping Up

Puppies naturally jump up to reach and greet their mother. Even after being separated from their mother, puppies will continue jumping up on people as a way to greet them. But jumping dogs may be annoying and can be dangerous as they can knock over an elderly person or child.

Jumping up is an attention-seeking behavior so the best method to stop your Poochon from doing this is by simply ignoring him. Do not look at your dog; just turn your back to him or walk away. Once your Poochon calms down and has all four paws on the floor, greet him calmly and reward his good behavior.

Begging

Begging is a bad habit, and often encouraged by pet owners. All dogs love food, especially table scraps. The best way to prevent your Poochon from begging in the first place is by never giving him food from the table.

If you cannot resist your Poochon's sad eyes while you are eating dinner or munching on pizza, take your pup to another room or to his crate and leave him there until you finish eating. Be sure to reward his good behavior after by placing a little snack in his food dish.

CHAPTER 6

Everything You Need to Know About House-training

House-training your Poochon requires consistency, patience and plenty of positive reinforcement. The goal is to train your pooch by instilling good habits and building a loving bond with him.

Typically, it will take four to ten months to completely house-train your Poochon. Since Poochons are a smaller breed, they have smaller bladders and faster metabolisms, which means more frequent bathroom breaks.

Photo Courtesy of Gillian Bull

Do not be discouraged by setbacks. Accidents are part of house-training. By being consistent, you can get your pooch on the right track in a few months' time.

Whether you are teaching a puppy or an older shelter dog, this chapter will answer all of your housebreaking questions.

Crate Training Basics

Some Poochon owners may feel guilty to be crate training their four-pawed best friend, but for your dog, the crate is his own private bedroom for resting and sleeping. All dogs instinctively search for small spaces to shelter themselves. A crate is more than a simple tool for potty training your Poochon. It will be your dog's safe haven and a lifesaver during emergencies.

Crate training is widely accepted by professional trainers and veterinarians as the most effective method to teach dogs desirable behaviors and preventing separation anxiety. Your Poochon will naturally accept his crate as his sleeping quarters and sanctuary, and generally speaking, most dogs avoid soiling their bedrooms.

When properly and humanely used, crate training provides many advantages for you and your Poochon:

Advantages for you

- You will have peace of mind when you have to temporarily leave your Poochon home alone, knowing your pup is comfortable and safe in his private bedroom, instead of running unrestrained throughout your house and, destroying who knows-what.
- By temporarily confining your Poochon to his crate, you can effectively establish a regular bathroom schedule, and prevent unwanted accidents during the night or when your pooch is left alone.
- Crate training will allow you to confine your Poochon when he becomes overly excited by guests or children running around. Another advantage is that you can temporarily place your dog inside of his crate during dinnertime which helps to prevent him from begging.
- You will be able to travel with your Poochon safely and be assured that your dog will quickly adapt to any new situations or strange surroundings, as long as he has his familiar "security blanket" - his crate.

Advantages for your dog...

- Your Poochon will love the privacy and serenity of having his own den, which he can retreat to whenever he is tired, not feeling well or is stressed out.

- Your dog's crate will spare your Poochon from feeling isolated, lonely, and frustrated from being placed alone in the basement or laundry room. The crate will only restrict him from certain things for his own safety and will not keep him away from his family surroundings.
- Your Poochon can be included in any family outings and trips instead of being left home alone.
- Since your Poochon will avoid soiling himself inside his crate, he will learn to control his bowels faster and associate elimination only within a specified location.

Since Poochons are highly social dogs, it is important that they are with you as much as possible, even if you are busy and cannot interact with them. Your Poochon needs to feel that he is part of your family. That comes from being included in family activities.

Although crate training is a fantastic training tool, it can be abused. Never leave your Poochon locked inside the crate all day long. Leaving a dog locked inside for long periods at a time is inhumane and cruel. This can

Photo Courtesy of Jo Shah

cause emotional distress or destructive behavior, not to mention physical harm. If your dog were to spend large amounts of time confined to his crate, he would likely start to exhibit problematic behaviors, such as barking, chewing, and jumping.

If your schedule requires you to leave your Poochon home alone all day, hire a dog sitter or ask a close friend to drop by every three to four hours to let your dog out of his crate. This will help him to stretch his legs, go to the bathroom and to play.

If your Poochon is under twelve months of age, he should never stay inside of his crate for more than two to three hours at a time. This is because your puppy cannot control his bladder and bowels for long periods of time.

Your Poochon's crate requires regular maintenance, otherwise, it can become soiled and become a breeding ground for bacteria. You will need to regularly wash your Poochon's bedding in hot water and disinfect his crate using pet-friendly cleaning supplies.

Be sure to remove any dangling ID tags, harnesses or collars which could easily get caught on the crate doors causing injury or accidental strangulation.

How to Crate Train

Even though dogs are considered den animals and prefer having a small space that's all theirs, Poochons often will not automatically take to their crate, as they prefer spending time with their families. If you do not handle crate training properly, your Poochon may even come to fear his crate. First introductions have never been more important!

If you follow the suggestions below, your Poochon will love his crate and may even start to go into the crate on his own whenever he needs some quiet time or rest.

First introductions

One of the worst ways to introduce your dog to his crate is by forcing him into it and locking him inside. You would not like to be trapped inside of a small, confined room, and your dog does not either. The goal with the crate is for your Poochon to view it as his own private bedroom which he can enjoy whenever he wants.

For the first introduction, place a soft, fluffy bed or blanket and a couple of chew toys in the crate and leave the door open. If you have a piece of blanket with your pup's mother's scent, be sure to place it in the crate, as it will be reassuring for your dog. While your puppy is watching, throw in a few treats, then back off and give your Poochon the space he needs to explore his crate on his own. Most Poochons will immediately go into the crate after the treats and start sniffing around.

If your Poochon is wary of entering his crate, try enticing him by placing his food dish, treats and favorite toys near and inside the crate. Your ultimate goal is to help your Poochon feel comfortable with going inside his crate. This could take a few days. Be patient with your puppy throughout the entire process.

Use during mealtimes

Once your Poochon freely enters and leaves his crate, your next goal is to get your dog comfortable with staying in the crate for longer periods of time. Use your Poochon's love of food to your advantage by creating a positive association with the crate by feeding him inside the crate. Try placing the food dish far back in the crate so your Poochon has to go all the way inside. If your Poochon is not willing to go all the way back, place his food dish towards the front of the crate. Each time you feed him, slowly move it back.

Closing the crate

Once your Poochon is happily eating his meals inside his crate, while standing with his back towards the door, it is time to start closing the door. While he is eating, close the door without locking it. Once your pooch is finished eating his food, immediately open the door. Each time you feed your dog, leave him inside with the door closed a bit longer, adding a minute or two each time.

If your Poochon begins to whine, open the door immediately and be sure not to leave him inside as long, the next time. However, if he whines the following time, do not open the door until he stops whining, otherwise you will teach him that whining equals an open door.

HELPFUL TIP

House-training in an Apartment

Because of their size, Poochons are a popular choice for people who live in apartments. But how do you house train your dog if you don't have a yard? There are several options available to you, one of which is called paper training. Paper training consists of training your puppy to eliminate on a specific area of paper or puppy pads. You can progressively decrease the size of this padded area until you've designated a single padded area for your puppy to relieve himself. Consistency is key, so try not to move your puppy's padded area while he's learning. Eventually, as your dog's bladder matures, you may be able to eliminate the padded area.

Extending crate time

Once your Poochon loves his crate, then it is time to start lengthening his time inside. Entice your Poochon inside with a few treats and a favorite toy. Once he is in the crate, then close the door. Spend a few minutes hanging out near the crate then move out of sight, by going into another room. This will get your Poochon used to being alone inside the crate with the door shut. When you return, do not open the crate immediately, instead sit beside the crate for a few minutes more. Slowly increase your dog's time inside of the crate, being sure to reward him after each crate training session.

Leaving and returning

Once your Poochon has mastered all of the above steps without whining, then he is ready for you to leave him for short periods of time. The key with this step is to avoid any excitement. Entice your dog into the crate with a treat and a favorite chewing toy. Once he is inside, quickly praise him for being such a good boy and close the door. Go about your business in the house, then go outside, shutting the door to the house behind you. When you come back inside, keep a low-key attitude and ignore any excited behavior your dog may be displaying.

If your Poochon starts to whine or paw at the door of his crate before being released, ignore him until he stops then let him out. Otherwise, you are just reinforcing bad behavior that will develop overtime into a habit.

Crating your Poochon at night

Be sure to take your Poochon to his designated bathroom spot before bedtime. Place the crate in your bedroom, hallway or somewhere near to where you are sleeping. If your Poochon is still a puppy, he will need to go to the bathroom every two to three hours, so you want the crate close enough to you to hear your dog when he starts whining. If your Poochon is older, you should place the crate close to you, so your dog doesn't associate his crate with being socially isolated. Once, your Poochon sleeps through the entire night without disturbances, then you can move the crate to another location.

If your Poochon whines or cries from inside his crate during the night, it might be difficult to discern if he is whining to go to the bathroom or whether he wants to be let out of the crate. Ignore him for a minute or two and, if he continues whining, use the word or phrase your dog associates with eliminating himself. If he gets excited, then take him to his designated bathroom spot.

If you are convinced that your Poochon is only whining so you let him out of his crate, do not give in. Ignore him until he stops whining, otherwise, you are teaching him by whining loudly that he can get what he wants. Never yell at your Poochon or tell him to stop whining and pound on the crate, as this will only make things worse.

Once your dog is comfortable with being left in the crate for fifteen minutes at a time, you can start leaving him inside for longer periods. If he is still a puppy and not housebroken, never leave him inside his crate for more than thirty minutes at a time. A full grown dog that is house-trained should never be left inside of his crate for more than four hours at a time.

Dos and don'ts of crate training:

Never punish your dog while he is inside the crate, otherwise he will associate his crate with negative experiences.

Never leave your dog inside the crate for more than four hours at a time. Crates are NOT substitute dog sitters. Leaving your dog locked inside for an extended period of time can cause separation anxiety and depression.

Do not make a big show over your departure. Place your dog inside the crate a few minutes before leaving and make sure he is occupied with a toy or treat before you leave.

Do take your dog to the bathroom as soon as you get home, as this will help your dog realize potty time comes after crate time.

House-training Basics

House-training your Poochon takes time, patience, commitment and vigilance. Your Poochon will most likely have several accidents in the house. This is a normal part of bringing home a puppy. However, by following the suggestions below, you will learn how to minimize potty accidents. It may take several weeks, even a few months to successfully train your Poochon.

Try to maintain the routine below for two to three weeks. If your dog stops having accidents in the house, you can start giving him a little more freedom each week. Reinforce good behavior by continually rewarding your Poochon for going on his designated spot.

Establish a routine and be consistent in sticking to the following suggestions:

Set a schedule - Puppies thrive on a regular schedule. Plan on taking your Poochon outside or to his designated bathroom spot inside the house frequently, at least every two hours, and as soon as he wakes up after his nap, after eating or playing. If your dog does not seem interested in going potty, restrict his access inside of the house and try again in fifteen minutes.

Reward good behavior - Generously praise your Poochon every time he relieves himself in his designated spot. Be sure to praise him and give him his treat immediately after going to the bathroom; do not wait until you are back inside.

Establish a location - Choose a convenient location inside your house or outside to be your Poochon's bathroom spot. If you clean up an accident inside of the house, after disinfecting the area correctly (as explained in the next section of this chapter), take the soiled paper towels and rags to the bathroom spot.The scent will help your Poochon recognize the area where you want him to eliminate. Below you can find more information about cleaning up after your Poochon.

Use a verbal cue - Before and while your dog is relieving himself, be sure to say the command word for bathroom – go potty – to remind him of the task at hand. Do not play with your dog until after he has relieved himself, as puppies get easily distracted and may forget they had to go to the bathroom until they go back inside the house and have an accident.

Regular feeding times - As soon as possible, get your Poochon on a regular feeding schedule. Depending on the instructions from the breeder, your Poochon may need to be fed two to four times a day. By feeding your dog at the same time each day, he will relieve himself more consistently, making house-training easier on both of you.

Bedtime - Just because it is bedtime, it does not mean that you can take a break from house-training. Take turns with a family member to get up every hour or two to take your puppy to the bathroom. Remember, his bladder is not fully developed yet, and he will not be able to hold it all night.

Supervise, supervise, supervise - Until your Poochon is fully house-trained, avoid letting him roam about your house freely, as it will reduce any opportunities to have an accident inside. Use baby gates or tether him with a long leash to prevent him from wandering around unsupervised.

Do not acknowledge bad behavior: If your Poochon has an accident, simply take him to his pad or litter box. Never yell at him or tell him he is a bad dog or give him another type of punishment. Clean up his mess using an enzyme-based cleaner. Remind yourself that the reason your dog had an accident is because you were not paying attention to his signs when he needed to go to the bathroom.

Cleanup on aisle K9 – It is inevitable that your Poochon will have an accident or two in the house, no matter how careful or diligent the training methods. If you catch your dog relieving himself indoors, do not scold or punish him. This can worsen the problem and cause your dog to feel anxious about going to the bathroom in front of you, causing him to search for hidden spaces to potty, making it even harder to break bad habits.

Cleaning up after doggy accidents

Puppy accidents can be a pain in the neck. However, they can easily be avoided if you clean up those accidents quickly, efficiently, and correctly.

Contrary to common belief, dogs do not relieve themselves in the house out of spite, or because they are impossible to train. The majority of potty accidents happen for one of the following reasons:

1. Your Poochon does not yet understand where he is supposed to go to the bathroom.
2. You are not giving your puppy ample and frequent opportunities to go to the bathroom on his designated spot.
3. Your pup suffers from a medical condition, which will be discussed below.

If you do not thoroughly clean and deodorize where your puppy had an accident, it will lead to more accidents in the same area. Simply wiping up the mess might satisfy your eyes and nose, but there is an enzymatic scent only your dog can smell that will lure him back to the same spot later on.

Follow this three-step cleaning process to deter any future potty accidents:

1. **Protect your own paws:** Before cleaning up your dog's mess, make sure to wear gloves to protect yourself from potential urine and fecal pathogens, especially if your Poochon is not fully vaccinated yet.
2. **Remove the mess:** For any type of accident, pick up any solids with a paper towel or baggy and blot up (do not rub) any excess liquid. Once you have removed the bulk of the mess, follow up by using damp towels or rags to gently blot away the rest of the smaller residue.
3. **Use a good enzymatic neutralizer for doggy accidents:** Avoid using any ammonia-based cleaning products as it may enhance the urine smell, which will make the spot irresistible for your puppy. The best cleaning products will not mask the scent or simply clean up the accident, but they will neutralize the enzymes that entice your dog to pee or poop in that same spot. Look for products that are specifically designed for cleaning up after dogs.

Photo Courtesy of Claire Hill

When house-training relapses

It can be frustrating to discover your well-behaved Poochon regressing to bad bathroom etiquette. However, there may be a good reason for your pup's behavior.

- **Medical problems** - Bathroom accidents can often be associated with physical issues such as urinary tract infections or parasite infections. Be sure to check with your veterinarian to rule out any possible physical problems.
- **Submissive/excitement urination** – Some Poochons, especially younger ones, may temporarily lose bladder control when they become overly excited. Often, this occurs during greetings or playtime. Involuntary urination or defecation is not a house-training issue, as your dog simply has no control over it and is unaware that he just soiled himself.
- **Hormonal behavior** – As your Poochon matures, he will have hormonal changes. Marking territory is a common behavior trait for both male and female dogs. If your dog is marking inside the house, then return to the first steps of house-training. If the problems persist, you can consider using a belly-band designed to prevent him from marking.

A belly band for dogs looks like a big Band-aid or diaper that wraps around your Poochon's rear girth. Often, the belly band has a waterproof shell with an absorbent liner which prevents any unwanted accidents in your house. Most styles are reusable and machine washable.

- **Fear or anxiety** – If your Poochon is afraid of loud noises such as fireworks or thunderstorms, he may lose control of his bladder and/or bowels. If this happens, try to isolate the sounds that frightened him and help him learn to associate good memories with those noises.
- **Climate changes** – Be proactive by observing your pup's bathroom habits. During the warmer summer months, he may spend more time outside. But on the other hand, during the colder winter months, your pup may need to be reminded of proper indoor bathroom etiquette.
- **New environment** - Just because your dog is housebroken in your house does not guarantee that he will know how to act when placed in a new setting. If you are traveling or visiting a friend's house, go back to the basic house-training methods until you can trust your Poochon again.

Tell-tale signs your Poochon needs to go to the bathroom

Young puppies – under the age of four months – do not have enough muscular control to hold the urine or feces. The instant they have to go to the bathroom, often they have already gone. If you wait for any tell-tale signs that your little Poochon has to go, you will be too late. Instead, you need to anticipate your puppy's needs.

As mentioned before, your baby Poochon will need a bathroom break as soon as he wakes up, or after munching a few treats. Puppies also will need to relieve themselves after a few minutes of playtime. You are much better off giving your Poochon too many potty breaks than too few, because the more often he has accidents inside, the harder it will be to housetrain your puppy.

No matter how old your Poochon is, he will need frequent bathroom breaks until he is fully housebroken. As your dog ages, there are some telltale signs that indicate he has to go to the bathroom. By learning to read your dog's body language, you can learn to tell when he needs to relieve himself. Watch for the following telltale signs to prevent accidents:

- **Sniffing the floor** – Dogs will sniff out an area to go potty and will look for a familiar scent. If your Poochon starts sniffing the floor or around your furniture, immediately take him to his designated area and praise him for going potty there.
- **Turning in circles while sniffing the floor** – Sniffing the floor might just mean your pup is searching for something to eat. If he starts turning around in circles while sniffing, however, then he probably has to poop. Pick him up as fast as you can and get him to his bathroom spot. Again, praise him for a job well done.
- **Barking, scratching or standing at the door** – Puppies generally are very vocal about when they need to go. If your Poochon starts barking and staring in the direction of the door or his pee pads, then take him to his spot immediately.
- **Whining** – If whining is combined with any of the above behaviors, your dog most likely needs to go potty. Younger dogs who still have not mastered housebreaking will often just sit and cry to tell you they need to go really badly.

Potty Pads vs. Litter Box

Although most Pochoon owners prefer to train their dog to relieve themselves outside, sometimes it is necessary to teach them to have an indoor bathroom spot. Perhaps, this is due to living on the seventeenth floor of an apartment building or having mobility issues that prevents you from taking your puppy outside constantly for bathroom breaks.

Generally, indoor potty training is recommended for owners whose Poochons will permanently be trained to go indoors, as it can be difficult to train your dog to go outside, once he has been taught to go indoors. Other owners opt to partially indoor house-train their Poochon – or at least, until he is old enough to control his bladder or bowels.

If you decide to house-train your Poochon to go indoors, you will need to be very consistent and clear with your pup so as to prevent confusion as to where his designated spot is. Outdoor potty-training often is easier because dogs can clearly observe the distinction between indoors and outdoors. Plus, with indoor house-training, your Poochon may have difficulty distinguishing the difference between the carpet and the potty pads.

Photo Courtesy of Poppy Bevan

Your Poochon will not automatically know that he is supposed to relieve himself on the potty pads, etc. The general rules for house-training methods using litter boxes, potty pads, newspapers or grass pads are the same.

How to use potty pads, grass pads or litter boxes to house-train your Poochon:

This is one of the easiest indoor house-training methods and can be combined with outside potty breaks. Create a small confinement area inside of your house using doggy gates or a puppy play pen. Place your dog's crate inside the confinement area with his bed, food, water dishes, and any chew toys. Place your Poochon's potty pads in a corner. As your dog becomes more reliable about using his potty pads, you can gradually increase his area until you can trust him to relieve himself on his potty pads.

Litter boxes - Litter boxes resemble cat litter boxes.The difference is that they are filled with odorless doggy litter. The raised sides create a clearly defined area, preventing spillage, just in case your Poochon tends to miss his target. Litter boxes are relatively easy to clean up. It is preferable to use litter designed specifically for dogs as it is made of larger bits and absorbs more urinary volume.

One of the main disadvantages to doggy litter boxes is that smaller dogs may be hesitant to crawl into the box, making house-training more of a challenge. Other dogs may decide to eat the litter or fling it all over the room.

Potty pads – Potty pads are super absorbent, disposable, and/or washable. These pads will protect your flooring and carpets. Some pads come with a built-in scent to entice your Poochon to use it as his bathroom spot. The lack of edges means there will be occasional spillage. One of the main disadvantages is the pads can be messy if you do not replace the old pad with a new one before saturation occurs.

If you choose to use potty pads, you can increase your chances of success by placing them inside a tray with a low edge instead of putting them directly on the floor. This will prevent the potty pad from sliding around and will help your dog make the distinction between the floor and his bathroom area. Another advantage to placing a tray under the potty pad is it will eliminate a common problem with dogs who place their front paws on the pad, while their back end is off the pad, making a mess, of course.

Grass pads - Grass pads resemble a litter box but with artificial turf that mimics the outside. Like litter boxes, they have raised sides to prevent urine from leaking on the floor. This option can be helpful if you are house-training your puppy to go outside, as it will help reinforce appropriate bathroom surfaces. The grass pads need to be regularly cleaned otherwise they become quite smelly.

Whether you choose a litter box, artificial turf or potty pads, you will need to train your dog to use it by literally taking him to the designated spot. Reinforce good behavior by praising him each time he goes in the right place. Be patient and never punish him.

Rewarding Positive Behavior

Rewarding positive behavior is also known as positive reinforcement and it is the preferred training method by trainers and breeders worldwide. All dogs, including your Poochon, repeat behaviors that are rewarded. For example, if your pup gets a yummy treat when you tell him to sit, he will most likely sit in the future.

However, rewarding positive behavior is not as simple as giving your Poochon a snack or two every time he does something to please you. If you want to successfully house-train your pooch, there are a few dos and don'ts you should follow.

Praise and reward your Poochon's good behavior immediately – Your Poochon's memory is short. If he urinates on his designated spot, then praise him immediately. Do not wait until you go back inside to praise him, as he will have already forgotten about going to the bathroom. By praising your pooch right away, he will be able to associate the good behavior with a reward, such as generous praise, affection and, of course, a treat or two.

Wean away from treats – Using treats as rewards is an excellent method to motivate your Poochon in the beginning, but over time, you should wean him off treats and replace them with praise and affection. This is essential since Poochons have a tendency to gain weight as they age and they do not need the extra calories from treats.

Don't punish your Poochon – Your Poochon will try to do everything in his power to please you, but he will have accidents. If he does, remind yourself that it was your fault for not getting him to his designated area soon enough, simply clean up the mess and get on with your life. If you punish your dog for urinating on the floor by yelling or hitting him with the newspaper, you are only teaching him to not relieve himself in front of you. This is one of the main reasons why some dogs tend to relieve themselves when left home alone.

Playpens and Doggy Gates

Raising Your Poochon is a full-time job, but nobody expects you to be able to watch him 24/7. Playpens and doggy gates are an excellent tool to keep your Poochon safe, secure, engaged and close to you at all times!

A playpen or doggy gate will confine your Poochon to a small area of your house and will prevent him from roaming freely about the house and getting into trouble. They can also be used to separate pets who have trouble getting along and to protect your furniture against damage from your teething puppy. Plus, they are a huge asset in house-training your curious Poochon, but there are a few points to consider before you buy a playpen for your pup.

- **Durable materials** - You want a pen or gate that is durable enough to withstand some chewing and strong enough to prevent your puppy from pushing his way out.
- **Size and height** – The pen or gate should be tall enough so your dog cannot jump or crawl out of it. If it comes with interlocking panels to expand or change the shape of the pen, that will factor in the full-grown size of your Poochon and allows you to use the playpen or gate throughout his life.
- **Your Poochon's escape abilities** – Your Poochon is part Poodle, so he is highly intelligent and perhaps a real Houdini in disguise. For this reason, you may need to consider a more heavy-duty gate or playpen with taller sides.
- **Easy set-up** – You will be moving the playpen or gate from room to room when you are house-training your Poochon, so it needs to be portable and easy to set up.

While choosing a playpen or doggy gate for your pooch, take into consideration the layout of your home. The majority of outdoor playpens can be used inside but the opposite is not always possible. Consider portability if you plan to travel with your Poochon's playpen or doggy gate or use it outside during the warmer months.

CHAPTER 7

Socializing Your Poochon

Socializing your Poochon is the key to ensuring you will have a happy, confident, and well-adjusted dog in the future. Also, it helps your pooch learn to be comfortable within his society which includes many different types of people, environments, buildings, sounds, sights, smells, animals and other dogs.

Properly socializing your Poochon early on in life ensures he does not spend his life jumping out of fright at anything that moves. Adult dogs who have not been properly socialized during there younger years often will be fearful or aggressive when exposed to something new.

Photo Courtesy of Takita Pyart

Importance of Good Socialization

The idea behind socializing your Poochon is to help him become acclimated to different types of sights, sounds, and smells in a positive, memorable manner. Proper socialization will prevent your pooch from being fearful of the mailman, children, car rides, etc. and help him develop into a well-mannered, happy companion.

HELPFUL TIP
Are They Kid-Friendly?

Poochons are generally considered to be kid-friendly dogs, but due to their size and activity level, they may be best suited to older children or children who are familiar with this kind of dog. Always be sure to supervise playtime between your kids and dog, and be sure that children are aware of proper handling and behavioral cues for your dog.

Younger Poochons naturally accept everyday things they encounter in their environment until they reach a certain age, then they start to be suspicious of things they haven't experienced yet. After the first few months, it will become more of a challenge to get your Poochon to accept new situations that may frighten him.

In general, well-socialized dogs are more enjoyable to be around. This is because they feel more comfortable in a wide variety of situations than a poorly socialized dog. They are less likely to be aggressive or fearful when presented with something new. Poorly socialized dogs can be a headache, as they often react with fear or aggression when they meet unfamiliar people, animals, dogs or even new experiences.

On the other hand, Poochons who are well-socialized, feel calm and relaxed around cars, honking horns, other dogs, crowds, veterinary clinics, etc. and are a joy to live with as they adapt quickly to every situation. Often, well-socialized pups have fewer health issues than dogs who are constantly stressed out by their surroundings.

The more positive new experiences your dog is exposed to, the better!

Socializing your Poochon is a big project and requires planning. It requires exposing your Poochon to a wide variety of sounds, animals, dogs, places, people and experiences to help him be comfortable later on in life. Take into consideration the type of lifestyle you plan to give your Poochon and make a list of any sights or sounds he might encounter on a regular day. For example, consider some experiences such as trains, garbage trucks, crowds, cats, crying infants, a schoolyard full of screaming children and more. While it might be impossible to expose your pooch to everything he might encounter in his lifetime, the more bases you cover the better.

When socializing your Poochon try the following:

- Introduce your Poochon to one new situation at a time. This will help to avoid overwhelming him. For example, if you plan a puppy play date, organize it in your backyard or a park your dog is already familiar with.
- Immediately, after a new experience or meeting a new person, reward your Poochon with a few treats and generous praise.
- If your Poochon seems uncomfortable or wary of the new experience, such as hearing a group of children playing in the playground, move further away and distract him by playing catch, moving gradually closer each time.
- Always follow any new socialization experiences with praise, patting, a fun game of catch and, of course, a special treat.

Socializing your Poochon is not optional. It is an essential part of your Poochon training. It will help him grow up into a relaxed and happy companion. The more well-adjusted your dog is to his surroundings, the easier it will be for you to share your life with him.

What is the best age for socializing your Poochon?

The best age to socialize your Poochon is between three and sixteen weeks old. After that age, your dog will become more wary and cautious of situations and things he has not encountered yet. From about sixteen to twenty weeks old, the opportunity to smoothly socialize your Poochon gets harder and harder. After twenty weeks old, it is more difficult to socialize your dog, but not impossible.

Since your Poochon has not received all of his vaccinations at this age, you should be careful when exposing your puppy to unknown animals or even walking in areas where animals might have been. However, if you wait to socialize your dog until he is old enough to be vaccinated, you might miss out on vital training opportunities.

If you have adopted an older Poochon, even though you may have missed out on the crucial puppy socialization period, it is not too late to teach an old dog new tricks.The key is slowly reintroducing your older Poochon to sights, sounds, smells, people and animals with careful supervision and a huge dose of positivity in the form of praise and treats. With patience you can help your Poochon overcome all of his fears.

How to socialize your Poochon during a pandemic

Due to the recent pandemic, families are home more than ever, which means your Poochon is drinking up all of the extra love and attention.

However, with social distancing and lockdown, your Poochon may be missing out on exposure to new situations, other dogs and animals, and meeting unfamiliar people.

Here are three steps to take to prepare your Poochon for when life returns to normal:

Socialize

Expose your Poochon to new experiences in or near your house every day. For example, drop a book, open an umbrella, wear a Mexican sombrero, stand outside and watch the garbage truck or walk on a street with heavy traffic (with your pup on a leash of course). Generously praise your Poochon after each new situation. These exercises teach your dog to stay calm when something out of the ordinary happens or there is a loud noise.

During a pandemic, it is less likely someone will approach you to pat your adorable Poochon. Even though strangers might not draw close to pat him and give him treats, you can still teach him that strangers are fun. While walking your Poochon, be sure to praise him and give him a treat every time you walk by someone on the street and keep doing this until the person passes. This exercise will teach your pup that people coming towards him is a positive experience.

Photo Courtesy of Kayla-Jade Harrison

Handling

During a pandemic, the majority of groomers are not open, and vet visits are kept to a bare minimum. Since your Poochon is not being handled by strangers as often as normal, it is up to you to get him used to being handled. Touch and closely examine his paws, nails, teeth, eyes, and underneath his tail at least three to four times a week. Brush your Poochon for five to ten minutes a day. Do not forget to praise your little puppy throughout the process and give him a treat or two.

People tend to pat dogs in many different ways, so get your Poochon used to a number of different ways of being handled by scratching him under the chin, patting his head, or by going against the grain of his hair. If he gets nervous at any point, stop and try again later on.

Photo Courtesy of Claire Hill

Routine

During a pandemic, the majority of pet owners are working from home, which is fantastic for a new puppy. Even though your life may be less structured than previously, your Poochon still needs a regular schedule to feel safe and secure. Your dog needs to play, eat, and nap the same time every day. This schedule should resemble your "normal life" and not the schedule you currently have.

Place your Poochon in his crate or playpen for at least two hours a day, while you and the rest of your family go to another part of the house. This exercise teaches your Poochon to be alone, preventing social anxiety later on in his life. If your Poochon gets agitated when you leave him alone, give him an extra special chew toy or bone that he can only chew on when he is alone.

Socializing Your Poochon with Other Dogs

Puppy classes are one of the best ways to give your Poochon a head start on learning how to act around other dogs. A typical class will teach your puppy how to interact, play and socialize with other dogs. Also, your Poochon will learn to trust people other than you, to touch, pat or handle him. Another advantage to these classes is that they lay a foundation for obedience training.

However, just a word of caution: Since your puppy has not received all of his vaccines yet, you will need to be extra careful when exposing him to unknown dogs or even walking in areas where other animals may have been. But on the other hand, if you wait until your Poochon is old enough to be vaccinated, you will miss out on crucial training opportunities.

By taking the following precautions when socializing your puppy, you almost completely eliminate the risks of him becoming sick:

- Before socializing your Poochon with another dog, ask the owner if their pup's vaccinations are up-to-date and if he is parasite-free.
- Avoid socializing your Poochon in dog parks or other areas. Organize a meet-and-greet with dogs in a controlled environment, such as your backyard or an area that can be easily disinfected.
- Sign your Poochon up for puppy training that specialize in socializing puppies.
- Taking your Poochon for daily walks is an excellent opportunity to burn off excess energy and expose him to other dogs in a neutral setting. Word of caution: Before introducing your Poochon to a new dog, ask the owner if their dog's vaccinations are up-to-date and if their pet is parasite-free.

Socializing your older Poochon with other dogs

As mentioned before, the best time to socialize your Poochon is while he is still a puppy. Unfortunately, it is not always possible to socialize your dog within this short time-frame. This is especially true if you have adopted an older Poochon and he never had a good opportunity to be socialized in the past. Or perhaps your Poochon was sick when he was a puppy and the veterinarian recommended to keep him away from other dogs.

Whatever may be the reason your Poochon was not taught how to behave around other dogs when he was younger does not mean he is a lost cause. The key is slowly reintroducing your older Poochon to sights, sounds, smells, people and animals with careful supervision and a huge dose of positivity in the form of praise and treats. With patience, you can help your Poochon overcome any fears.

Here are some tips on how to socialize your adult Poochon:

Introduce your dog to dogs while walking – Walking your older Poochon is an excellent opportunity for your dog to observe and possibly meet other dogs, also to practice proper behavior when out and about.

Use a muzzle, if necessary – If your Poochon typically barks and growls at other dogs, then maybe you want to consider placing a muzzle on your Poochon. The muzzle will prevent your dog from biting or attacking another dog, and it will also help both dogs stay calmer and more receptive to meeting each other.

Expose your Poochon to different social activities – Instead of taking your unsocialized Poochon to the dog park and hoping for the best, expose him slowly by walking your pooch while on the leash around the outside of the park, letting your dog observe the dogs play inside. Take your time, introduce your Poochon to a new situation each day and be sure to generously praise and reward him for any good behavior.

Introducing Your Poochon to Your Resident Dog

One of the biggest mistakes pet owners make when introducing their new dog to their older resident dog is simply tossing them together and hoping for the best.

Your older resident dog has already declared your house his territory. When you bring a new dog into the older resident dog's territory, he may respond with aggression to defend what he feels is rightfully his. Depending on your new Poochon's energy level and personality, he may be submissive, act fearful, or even fight back.

According to the Humane Society, more than forty percent of US households that have pet dogs have more than one dog. The majority of those dogs in a multiple-pet household did not arrive at the same time. So, if you are bringing your Poochon into your pack, what are the dos and don'ts of the first introduction?

Choose a neutral area – Ask a friend or family member who knows your older dog for assistance. You, your new Poochon, your helper and your current dog should meet in a neutral area, such as a place where you do not walk your resident dog often and that is not familiar to your new dog.

Go for a walk together – Go for a long walk together, as it will drain both dogs' energy levels and allow them to become familiar with each other in a place that is neither of their territories. Once the dogs walk together side by side, tolerating each other, then you can go home. First, enter the house with your current dog, and then bring in the new dog inside of your house. By doing this, your resident dog is essentially inviting the new dog into his territory as his guest.

Use a leash – Introduce your new Poochon to your current dog while on the leash. This will allow the older dog to feel as if he is in control of the situation. Also, if there are altercations, you can quickly pull your puppy out of harm's way without causing a huge commotion.

Photo Courtesy of Leanne Patel

Do not place the dogs in the same crate – This is a recipe for disaster. Do it this way, and you will wind up with one or both dogs being injured, and some very hurt feelings. Instead, close off a small part of the house with either a dog gate or playpen with the new dog's crate inside.

Do not get involved – Once your dogs are both inside the house together, there may be altercations between the two of them, but do not become irritated or annoyed with your older dog. It is natural that the older dog will try to put the new dog in his place. Stay calm and let them establish hierarchy among themselves.

Do not forget to show affection to your older dog – Small puppies can be quite annoying for older dogs and they can feel a tad-bit jealous of the attention you are giving the new dog. Do not forget to cuddle your older dog with extra love and attention to reconfirm that you still love him. Do not expect the dogs to embrace each other instantly; often it can take up to six months before the new addition to the household is accepted or tolerated.

Helpful suggestions to ease the tension between your dogs:

- Confine your Poochon to an established part of the house which is far away from the older dog's crate and feeding area. Be sure to make any changes at least a week before bringing home your new dog and allow your older dog to sniff out the new dog's area.
- After your dogs have finished eating or play time, place your new puppy inside his crate and close the door. Ask your older dog to come over and investigate the new dog on his own terms.
- Give your older dog the royal treatment! This will prevent his feelings from being hurt. Never let the new dog push past him for your affection or praise. Your older pet deserves and needs to feel he is still loved as much as he was before.

Cats and Dogs

Typically, cats are more aloof and distrustful while dogs are generally more sociable and territorial. However, these differences do not indicate that dogs and cats cannot share the same space – they simply need a little help from you.

With some simple training techniques, love and a whole lot of patience, your Poochon and cat may eventually become friends or at least tolerate each other.

Here are some suggestions to help your Poochon and your cat get along:

Use positive reinforcement - Never yell at or hit your cat or dog, as it will just make the situation even more uncomfortable, tense, and stressful. Instead, reinforce any type of positive behavior between each other, such as tolerating each other from different sides of the room. Offer treats for any type of good behavior around each other. Reinforcing good behavior when they are relaxed will lead to them wanting to be around each other, as they will learn that this means receiving praise, treats, and affection from you.

Play games together - Never under-estimate the power of playtime, especially if it encourages your beloved pets to play together. Play games with each pet separately, with the other pet within a close proximity to observe. Once your cat and dog appear to tolerate each other, even if it is from a distance, play games with each one simultaneously such as playing with a string, hide-and-seek or scavenging games. Just a word of caution - Be careful not to play any games that may get either pet overly excited or hyper.

Give them their space - Even though you want your Poochon and cat to be best buds, it is never the best decision to force them together. Instead keep your cat and dog separated if there is any sign of aggression, fighting or stress. Cats and dogs need some time and space apart from each other during an argument.

Keep them safe - While teaching your Poochon and cat to like each other, you need to take into consideration their physical safety. For first introductions, you will want to play it safe instead of sorry, as you do not really know how either of your pets will react. Provide high places for your cat to run to and for your dog, use two levels of safety such as a leash and a baby gate. If your pup gets too excited, ask him to lie down or distract him with his chew toy.

Use sensory cues - Cats and dogs are both highly scent-oriented. Swap out beds, blankets or towels to help your dog and cat get used to each other's scent without the pressure of seeing one another. Another helpful sensory cue is to let them listen to each other's sounds from a safe, comfortable distance, so when they are closer together, a bark, growl or hiss will not frighten the other pet.

Give your cat his own territory

Cats need to feel safe and protected.

Set up a "base camp" by making a refuge that your Poochon cannot access. Create several safe spots for your cat around the entire house to allow your cat to confidently navigate the shared space without crossing paths with his canine roommate.

All cats are natural climbers, so take advantage of your home's vertical space to create an escape route for your cat. Install shelves, buy tall cat trees, or place a cat bed on top of a bookcase. By doing this you give your cat an opportunity to observe your Poochon from a safe distance of his choice.

Make sure your Poochon cannot access your cat's litter box. Cats enjoy privacy while doing their business, plus some dogs enjoy snacking on cat feces, which is a bad habit for your Poochon because he can contract intestinal parasites. These parasites can cause a long list of health problems, such as vomiting, diarrhea, anemia, and weight loss.

Baby gates are an excellent option to keep your Poochon out of your cat's base camp, but since Poochons are known for being escape artists, keep the litter box in an open space and use an uncovered box. This way, your cat will not be surprised and cornered mid-squat.

To prevent disastrous mealtime encounters, schedule regular mealtimes for your cat and dog, in other words - no free feeding. Place bowls at separate ends of the house or place your cat's food dish up high on a table or countertop where your Poochon cannot find it.

Keep a close eye on your cat's toys. Dogs tend to love the scent of catnip even more than cats, which can prompt competitive fighting and bickering.

The following steps will maximize the chances for success:

- Before you bring home your Poochon, make sure your cat is up-to-date with her vaccinations and is parasite-free. Plan to keep your pets separated for at least three days after the new arrival. The goal is for your cat to get used to your dog's presence without face-to-face contact. Even though they cannot see each other, they can smell and hear each other.
- Feed your cat and dog on opposite sides of a closed door. This will help your cat to associate the presence of the new dog with something pleasant, such as eating. If your cat seems skittish about eating close to the door, then place her food dish a few feet away and slowly move it closer each day or until your cat is comfortable eating next to the door.
- Begin face-to-face meetings in the common area of your house. Keep your Poochon on a leash and distracted with a chew toy and let your cat come and go as she wishes. Do not restrain either pet as that could result in injury. Reward your cat with treats and praise then do the same with your dog. If either pet shows signs of aggression, redirect your pet's attention by tossing a play toy, etc.
- Be prepared to supervise your pets' interactions for at least the next few weeks, perhaps even longer.

Do not be surprised if there are altercations. If the cat growls or bats his paws at the dog, it is his way of communicating his boundaries to the dog. With time, the cat will learn to co-exist with the new dog.

Just as you would with an older resident dog, reassure your cat that you love him by patting him and giving him some of his favorite snacks. Cats like to do things on their own terms so never force your cat to meet-and-greet the new dog as it will not end well.

Realize your cat has a personality. If he acts like he just barely tolerates the new dog, then that means that he probably has accepted your Poochon. Remain watchful, to ensure all of their interactions go smoothly – especially when your Poochon hits his rambunctious "teenage" stage.

Socializing with Other Animals

Do you have smaller pets, such as hamsters, rabbits, guinea pigs, gerbils, geckos, etc.?

While dogs usually consider small animals as prey rather than buddies, the two species can live together peacefully. Before you introduce your Poochon to your small critters, it would be helpful if your dog has previously learned some basic commands such as sit, come, and stay. These commands will guarantee your Poochon will be well-mannered and make a good first impression with your small critter.

Prior to their first introduction, take your Poochon out for an invigorating walk and a game of fetch to tire him out. A hyperactive and overly excited dog can frighten your small pet.

After your Poochon is worn out from playtime, confine your small critter to its cage, which is its safe space. Bring your Poochon close while on a leash. Command him to Sit and Stay next to the cage and reward your dog for any calm, non-aggressive behavior. Allow him to sniff at your small critter through the cage, then reward him once again for any good behavior. If your dog tries to snap or bark at the small critter moving freely in his cage, walk away with your dog and try again later.

After the initial introduction, continue having your pets meet for a few minutes at a time, lengthening the time of each meeting. Always keep your Poochon on a leash and your small critter confined until your dog shows no sign of aggression. Once this happens, let your small critter run about its enclosure freely while your Poochon observes on his leash. When your dog neither shows any interest in chasing after the critter nor displays any signs of aggression, then you can try letting him off his leash. Never forget to praise and reward your dog's good behavior.

Poochons are half Poodle, who were originally bred to hunt small animals, so a small rodent such as a rabbit, guinea pig, or hamster is an almost irresistible temptation. Even if your dog shows no signs of aggression or prey drive around your small critter for an extended period of time, he could still harm it, even by accident. Never ever leave your Poochon unsupervised with your small critter.

Options if Your Pets Don't Get Along

Every pet owner's dream is to come home and find their pets cuddled up together on their blanket. Yet, the sad reality is pets do not always get along, especially if they are different species. If you find your two pets cannot be friendly, they may need to be separated for a few days, then reintroduced to each other.

Reasons why your pets may not be getting along:

Hormonal - Often disagreements between your pets are related to hormonal changes. An easy fix for this problem is to make sure all of your resident pets are spayed or neutered, as this will keep any unwanted aggression at bay.

Food - All animals, no matter their species, have a built-in instinct to protect their food. If you notice aggression around mealtimes, place your pets' food dishes in separate parts of the house and feed them at the same time.

Jealousy - All pets need to feel loved and cherished. An easy solution for this problem is to designate quality time with each of your pets alone, without the other pets watching. This will ensure each pet that you love it and are never going to replace them.

Dominance - Rivalry among pets is normal, especially if you bring a new pet into the household. Only one pet can be the leader of the pack, and this is something they need to figure out on their own terms and time schedule. Once, your pets have established which pet is the leader, respect their decision by feeding the boss first.

Fights will happen, especially during the first few weeks as they determine who will be the dominant leader in the house. When this happens, never attempt to separate them, as you will end up injuring yourself. The best solution is to douse the animals in water, causing them to back off from each other instantly. Be sure to keep them separated and under close supervision until they learn to get along.

A good relationship between your pets may only take a few days to build or it could take a couple of years. Managing their environment and using

Photo Courtesy of Adline Jeyakumar

positive reinforcement will help your pets to get along and is an essential part of the process.

If you fear your pets' behavior towards each other may cause harm to each other, you or even another person, it is not unreasonable to think about giving up one of your pets. Some pets cannot and will not tolerate other pets and are happier living in an "only child" environment.

But, before you consider such a drastic decision, there are lots of behavior specialists out there who are willing to extend you a helping hand to encourage your pets to get along. A certified dog or cat trainer or a board-certified veterinary behaviorist will be able to diagnose and treat your pets' stress, anxiety, phobias, aggression, and reactivity towards each other. Often extreme misbehavior occurs because the pet is suffering from an underlying medical condition, so be sure to check with your vet.

Talk to friends and family members

Maybe you have decided to give up one of your pets, but perhaps your cousin would love to adopt him. Or a colleague could be searching for a furry companion. If you just ask around, you will be surprised how many people would be thrilled to give your pet a new forever home. Just be sure the home is suitable for your pet by visiting ahead of time.

Seek out rescue groups

Most localities have active rescue groups dedicated to "fostering" pets in a caring loving home until they can find them their forever home. One of the main advantages to a rescue group is you are assured that your pet is going into a home of someone who not only loves pets but understands how to take care of them. There is also the option of looking for rescue breed-specific groups.

Find a "no-kill" organization or shelter

If you are considering surrendering your pet to a shelter, you absolutely need to confirm that it is a "no-kill" facility. These types of shelters have the goal of helping your pet find a new loving, forever home as soon as possible.

Ask around

If you did not have luck with the above alternatives, then think outside of the box and contact dog trainers or your veterinarian to see if they know of any good homes who are searching for a good pet. For anybody who genuinely cares about their pets, the pound is not even an option.

Poochons and Strangers

Even the friendliest dog can become aggressive if he is not properly socialized. To avoid this happening to your Poochon, you will need to expose him to as many different types of people as possible. But the quantity of those experiences is not as crucial as the quality of each of these encounters. Your pooch needs to associate each encounter as a positive, fun-filled experience.

Socializing your Poochon involves exposing him to as many different people as possible, including men, women, children of all ages, men with beards, people in wheelchairs, and so on. You should also plan on introducing him to people wearing different styles of clothes such as uniforms, raincoats, hats and gloves, etc. If your Poochon has not received all of his vaccines, plan a meet-and-greet party at your house for him by inviting friends and family over.

If your Poochon only spends time with you and your immediate family, over time he can become wary of anyone who is NOT his family. For this very reason, it is crucial you diversify your pup's social calendar and organize a meet-and-greet.

When you take your Poochon out of his comfort zone, make sure you are relaxed and calm, as your dog can read your emotions. If you are nervous, then your pooch will be nervous too, and perhaps even afraid of the new situation.

Remember Rome was not built in a day – take your time introducing your Poochon to everyone on your list. Start off slow, first with friends and family then integrate a stranger, such as the postman. Avoid taking him to busy public areas too soon, as he may become overly excited or fearful of strangers in general.

Before introducing your Poochon to somebody new, inform them ahead of time that you are bringing your dog over for a brief, socialization session. Ask them to be ready to pamper him with love and affection and be sure to slip them a treat or two to give your dog.

Start off with meeting people in neutral, familiar environments, not a music festival or a parade which can be overwhelming for you and your pooch. Instead, plan your meet-and-greet while on your walk together, in your yard or at a dog-friendly café or in a small store. Once your Poochon has climatized to these situations, you can try standing outside of a busy supermarket with more people.

Here are some helpful suggestions to help your Poochon become acclimated to all sorts of people:

- Stay calm and confident during meet and greets, even more so if your Poochon is frightened. If your dog is skittish or agitated, don't make a big deal about his behavior as it will cause him to become more upset.
- When asking strangers to pat your Poochon, ask them to pat him where their hands can be seen, such as his chest or under his chin.
- Use treats and praise to give your Poochon a positive association with meeting strangers and experiencing new situations.
- Enlist a different dog-walker or dog-sitter each week to expose your Poochon to a variety of caregivers during the day.

Your Poochon should be exposed to the following people within his first few months with you:

- Neighbors
- Family and friends
- Groomer and vet
- Unfamiliar people wearing different styles of clothes (hoods, jackets, face masks, sunglasses, uniform, hats, and so on)
- Postman
- Anyone who regularly comes to your house

When organizing these different encounters, be sure to choose a variety of different environments for each one, such as shopping center, parks, inside of a store, etc. Your Poochon will want to investigate any foreign objects, such as wheelchairs, bicycles, skateboards, and benches.

Follow your Poochon's cues. Interactions should be long enough to make a positive impression, but not so long that you wear your buddy out. Even simple new experiences can be overwhelming for your puppy, so keep them short and sweet!

Poochons and Children

Poochons adore children of all ages. Plus, your Poochon's high energy can keep up with the energy of children. Poochons are very loving and gentle, making them an excellent fit for families with children. However, remember first impressions make lasting impressions and this statement cannot be truer when introducing your dog to children.

There are several benefits for children to be raised in a household with a dog, from improved social skills to teaching them responsibility. Studies have shown dogs can improve a child's mental health, and many children view their pet dog as their best friend in whom they can confide.

Similarly, your Poochon can benefit from the enthusiasm and energy of a younger playmate to keep him busy throughout the day. But even if you do not have children living in your house, your Poochon will need to learn to behave around children.

Dogs and children need to be properly prepared for first introductions and taught proper manners. If adequate training and supervision do not take place, it may create a dangerous situation for both the dog and child. As an overly enthusiastic child can easily injure your tiny Poochon. Likewise, a scared or overly excited puppy could bite and seriously hurt a child. However, these tragedies can be easily avoided if you are willing to put in the time to properly socialize your Poochon with children.

Educating children on proper behavior around your Pochon

Before introducing your Poochon to small children, sit down with them to establish a few ground rules about how to behave around your dog. It might be a challenge to get them to concentrate as children may have difficulty focusing when they are excited, so you might need to repeat the rules a few times.

- They should pat the dog gently.
- Never force attention on the dogs, instead let the dog come to them.
- The dog's crate is not a play toy or a place for hide-and-seek. It is strictly off limits. If the dog goes inside, leave him alone.
- Do not approach the dog while he is eating or chewing a bone.
- Leave the puppy alone while he is sleeping.

Make sure there always is an adult around to supervise interactions. Young children should never be left unattended with your Poochon.

Children can often mistake your adorable Poochon for a cuddly, stuffed toy, so it is important to remind them how to properly handle your dog. A general rule of thumb is to teach them to treat the puppy as they would another child; do not pull his ears or tail, climb on them, and engage in rough play. Here are some suggestions to consider when socializing your dog with children:

Create a positive environment – Before first introductions, make sure everyone is in a good mood. Never encourage a grumpy, cranky child to meet your Poochon or vice versa, as it is a recipe for disaster. Also, if the child is overly excited or rowdy, wait until he calms down – otherwise your Poochon will be scared.

Take it slowly – Children tend to have jerky movements and high-pitched voices when they get excited, which can easily frighten your Poochon. Before first introductions, show the children how to walk, talk, and approach your puppy. Tell them to use their inside voices and use gentle hands while patting the dog. No poking, grabbing, pulling, or squeezing the puppy. Keep introductions short and sweet!

Supervise – The first few introductions will be brief, but over time the dog and the children will adjust to each other's presence and be able to play together for longer periods. No matter how well they get along, never leave small children alone with your dog without proper supervision. Accidents happen quickly and it is crucial you are there to prevent them.

Let your Poochon set the pace – If your Poochon is nervous around children, let him set the pace. Instead of handing your puppy to the child to hold, ask the child to sit on the ground and place your Poochon near to him. Ask the child to play with something and your curious Poochon will come and investigate. As your Poochon's confidence grows, let the child pat him and eventually hold him.

Keep it positive – One of the best ways to build a good relationship between your Poochon and small child is by using positive reinforcement. When your pup is behaving properly around small children, generously praise him and give him lots of treats. This will teach your dog that good things happen whenever children are around. Soon he will seek out the children and be on his best behavior.

Safe spaces calm fears – One of the disadvantages with children and puppies is that they can easily get excited, which may cause misunderstandings and hurt feelings. It is important to teach your children that your Poochon's crate is his private place; if he goes there, it is because he wants some down time. Place your dog's crate in a secluded area of the house where he can retreat from the rambunctious children if he feels overwhelmed.

Steps for a successful first encounter with small children:

For the best success with his first encounter with a small child, choose a moment when your Poochon is tired, perhaps after a walk or playtime.

1. Ask the child to sit on the floor with his legs crossed. Place your Poochon nearby and have the child place his hand out with a treat for the puppy.
2. Once the puppy sniffs out the little person, you can gently pick up your puppy and place him on the child's lap. Remind the child to use his inside voice and to talk softly. Generously praise your Poochon and give

him a reward. Instruct the child to gently pat the puppy using soft, gentle strokes.

3. Your Poochon most likely will curl up and go to sleep. If not, he will decide to move on and explore his surroundings. If the latter happens, tell the child not to grab or pull the puppy back to his lap. Doing so could frighten and maybe even, hurt your small Poochon.
4. If your puppy decides to explore his surroundings, let him do so for a minute or two, then direct his attention to the child by repeating steps one and two. If the dog runs away again, be sure to reassure the child that the puppy likes him, but he is very curious.
5. Do not forget to praise and reward your puppy every time he sits and plays with the child. Positive reinforcement is the key to laying a healthy foundation for a healthy relationship between your Poochon and children of all sizes.

Socializing your Poochon is a life-long process that will need to be reinforced throughout the years. Never ever force interactions with strangers, other dogs or animals and children. Always let your dog establish his own terms for discovering and accepting new situations, environments and people.

CHAPTER 8

Puppy Parenting

Being a puppy parent is a big responsibility.

The goal with training your Poochon is to shape his behavior and teach him how to respond to certain phrases or commands.

Common Puppy-Parenting Mistakes

There is lots of information available about how to train your dog. You can basically teach your Poochon to do anything, if you have the time and patience. However, there are many common mistakes pet owners make while trying to train their four-pawed companions. These mishaps can have a huge impact on whether or not your training efforts are successful.

In order to avoid frustration on both ends of the leash, here are some universal mistakes to avoid.

Photo Courtesy of Tanya Zahedi

Waiting too long to start training – You should start training your Poochon from the moment you bring him home with you, regardless of age. The longer you wait to start training, the harder it will become. Young puppies may not be capable of learning advanced commands such as roll over, but you should be able to start on house-training immediately and teach basic commands such as sit, come and no.

Car rides – Does your Poochon dread car rides? Perhaps, it is because the only time he goes in the car is when he goes to the vet's office or to the groomer to be poked at by strange people. Regularly take your Poochon for car rides, to fun places such as the park, beach, pet store or even a doggy playdate at a friend's house. Do not forget to generously praise and reward your Poochon's good behavior.

Neglecting to socialize – Many pet-owners start off socializing their pooch but slowly lose interest. Socializing your dog with other dogs and people is an ongoing process. During the colder months, keep your Poochon well-socialized by organizing playdates with other dogs or enroll him in obedience classes.

Table scraps – Your Poochon's dark eyes can melt anyone's heart. Resist the temptation of feeding your pooch table scraps under the table or people food of any kind. Once your dog learns to beg for food, it is almost impossible to break this habit. Also, human food is often unhealthy for dogs and may cause future digestive issues. In chapter eleven of this book, you can find a list of toxic human foods.

Inconsistency – If you are inconsistent in training your dog, you will only confuse him. For example, say you make a rule that your Poochon is not allowed to sit on the couch. But occasionally you make an exception and let him sit with you. Then, you get upset when you come home from work and find your dog on the couch. He will not understand why sometimes he is allowed and then, not the next time.

Lack of patience – Training your Poochon takes time, so try not to get stressed out or frustrated. This will only make things even worse because your dog will also become agitated. If your Poochon is struggling to learn something, ask yourself if this is a good time to learn something? Or perhaps, the training session has gone on too long? Remember training sessions need to be short and sweet, approximately five to fifteen minutes.

Harsh punishment – Yelling, hitting, leash jerking and grabbing from the scruff of the neck are all forms of harsh discipline and have negative consequences. The training session should help you bond with your puppy, not be a bullying session. For example, you wake up and discover your Poochon had an accident on the carpet. Overreacting or scolding your dog will only confuse him. He has already forgotten about going to the bathroom on the carpet. Be patient and remember that he is still learning.

Reinforcing wrong behavior – One of the most common mistake pet owners make in dog training is accidentally reinforcing bad behaviors. All dogs are social creatures who seek our attention and approval. Any type of attention, whether positive or negative, is interpreted by your dog as your approval. For example, if your Poochon does something undesirable, such as jumping up on you, begging, or whining, the best thing to do is to simply ignore him until the behavior stops.

Not enough sleep – Puppies need plenty of sleep to stay healthy, happy and stimulated. When your Poochon becomes overtired or exhausted, he can become irritable, hyperactive, and even aggressive. If your pooch is under the age of six months, he needs an early bedtime and regular naptime in a safe, quiet designated sleep area.

Photo Courtesy of Angela Marshall

Photo Courtesy of Jenny Choudhury

How do you become the Alpha?

Wild canines and wolves operate as a social hierarchy, with one leader and his or her followers. Often, the alpha leader is the strongest of the pack, and makes the majority of the decisions for the rest of the pack. Just because your Poochon is domesticated does not mean that his hierarchical instinct has disappeared.

If you have more than one dog in your house, you may have noticed how one of the dogs seems to set the tone over the rest. Regardless of how many dogs you have in your house, there should only be one alpha in the home – YOU!

Being the alpha leader does not give you or anyone the right to punish or physically hurt your dog. By being the leader, you are simply establishing that your rules protect your dog. A word of caution: If you lose your patience and get visibly upset with your dog, in the eyes of your Poochon, you have already lost your position as the alpha leader.

Smaller breeds, like the Poochon, tend to gravitate towards whoever is in charge. However, you should be aware that during your pup's adolescent years, he will test your dominance before he decides to be a submissive, obedient dog.

Establish the rules and limitations – Poochons are part poodle, so their intelligence will urge them to test out limitations and challenge your authority. Never punish your dog; instead, firmly correct any bad behavior, such as jumping up on the couch or grabbing a piece of food from your hand.

Smaller dogs like your Poochon will whine until you pick them up. Do not pick him up until he stops whining or you have distracted him with another acceptable behavior.

Be consistent – Have a family meeting with everyone in your household to decide on the ground rules for your Poochon and make sure everyone is diligent in enforcing them. If you are not consistent, you will never see the results you want. In order for your dog to learn good behavior, he needs to identify consistent patterns.

If your Poochon is going to understand what is expected of him, the entire family needs to be on the same page. If one person says, "Sit" and another says, "Sit-Down," your puppy is going to be very confused, and it will take twice as long to teach him this command.

Stay calm yet assertive – In nature, the leader of the pack, or alpha dog, shows his dominance by taking charge of every situation. He is not nervous or doubtful. Your dog can sense your emotions. If you are uncertain or fearful, your Poochon will interpret it as a sign of weakness. He will think he needs to protect you and become your leader.

If he starts chewing on your furniture, say a firm NO. Then distract him with a more appropriate chew toy. Once he is chewing on the toy, praise and reward him.

Set a routine – Poochons love routine! The structure of a well-established routine teaches them what to expect each day. Be consistent in feeding, walks, playtime, bedtime and bathroom breaks. Your pup will benefit from an established routine, as he will not need to worry about what is – or is not – about to happen next.

Sticking to a regular bathroom schedule while house-training will prevent accidents in the house. If a dog feels a certain urgency to go to the bathroom, he is more likely to "hold it" if he knows and trusts that you are going to be giving him an opportunity soon to relieve himself.

Positive Reinforcement

Positive reinforcement is one of the most effective ways to train your Poochon. When using this method, you will give your pooch a reward to reinforce good behavior. For example, you ask your Poochon to "Sit," and he immediately does it, you give him a treat. You are rewarding his good behavior.

Positive reinforcement teaches your dog that positive actions equal rewards. This reward can be in the form of verbal praise, affection by scratching behind his ears, a game of fetch, or a delicious treat. Your dog's brain observes the cause and effect. Your dog's brain saying, "If I sit, I get spoiled! Wow, I need to sit every time they ask me!" And practice makes perfect.

It might take a few practice sessions for your Poochon to notice the pattern of COMMAND + OBEDIENCE = REWARD. If you want to get the most out of positive reinforcement training, there are a few Do's and Don'ts to follow:

Immediately reward your Pochoon's good behavior
Your Poochon has a short attention span and lives in the moment, so your response to his good behavior should be immediate. You can reward your dog, using both praise and treats, whenever your dog's behavior pleases you. For example, if you are house-training your Poochon, be sure to reward him every time he does his business outside.

Keep sessions short and fun
The goal is to teach your Poochon that good things happen when he obeys you. Make training sessions short, fun, and positive - leaving each class on a good note. For example, if your Poochon has difficulty learning a new command, end the session by asking him to perform a command he already has mastered.

Wean from treats
Treats are an excellent tool to motivate your Poochon, in the beginning, but you will eventually want to wean him off all of those extra treats and switch to more praise and affection. Over time, your dog will forget about those high calorie treats and just want to please you.

Don't make it complicated
Keep commands simple and clear. Instead of teaching your Poochon to "*Sit Down Here*," simply say "*Sit*." Choose specific and simple commands.

Don't be inconsistent
It is useless to reward your dog for staying off the couch but then later let him come on the couch for a cuddle. This type of behavior will confuse your Poochon and he will not be able to decipher what you actually want. Additionally, everyone in your household needs to understand and abide by the rules for your dog, otherwise he may run himself ragged trying to figure out how to behave with each member of your family.

Stop correcting your Poochon
Many pet parents assume that positive reinforcement means they cannot say no to their dogs. This is not true. If your Poochon is acting out of sorts, a firm NO is one of the best ways to correct his bad behavior. Of course, you should never yell, scold, hit, grab or hurt your Poochon in any way.

How to reward your Poochon

Knowing which rewards to give your Poochon can make training sessions more stimulating and fun for both you and your dog. Here are several ways to reward your pup's good behavior:

Treats

Treats are one of the most popular rewards for positive reinforcement, as they are fast and easy to dispense. Plus, it is gratifying to see our little four-pawed companion happily devour his snack. Treats are ideal for training sessions with your Poochon when you are teaching him to learn a new behavior or command. However, the downside to treats is they are high in calories, which can be an issue if your Poochon has a weight problem.

Games

Often pet owners forget that games are another fun way to reward your Poochon. Initiate a game your dog enjoys immediately after your dog does something which pleases you. Games stimulate your dog's brain in the same way as yummy treats. For example, ask your pooch to sit, and once he sits, offer him the ball and start playing fetch. During the game you can teach him the command Leave It or Drop It. Once he drops the ball, tell him to sit down again and when he does, start playing fetch again. Your Poochon will love this method to reinforce proper behavior.

Praise and attention

There is nothing your Poochon loves more than being praised and getting attention from you. A pat on the chest or a scratch under the ears is just

Photo Courtesy of Caitlin Murphy

as rewarding for your dog as a handful of treats. Instead of giving him your undivided attention, make him work for it first. For example, ask him to sit down. Once he does what you have requested, then give him some cuddle time. If he does not do what you requested, then walk away and when you return, try again. This exercise teaches your pooch that certain actions either get him attention or not.

Clicker Training – It Really Works

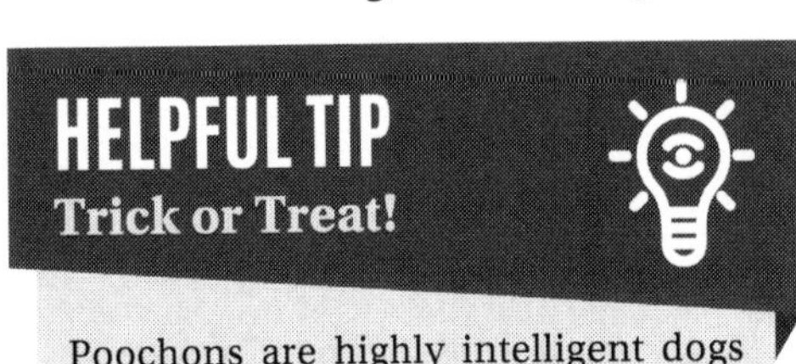

Poochons are highly intelligent dogs and need plenty of mental stimulation to stay entertained and out of trouble. Teaching your Poochon tricks is not only a fun project for you, but it's also a great way to entertain your dog! With positive reinforcement and some treats, your Poochon is likely to catch on to new tricks quickly.

Clicker training began in the late 1990s as an effective alternative to negative training methods that relied heavily on pain, fear, or intimidation to basically bully a dog into being obedient. Clicker training is often combined with positive reinforcement methods and is considered to be a highly effective teaching option.

A clicker is a small, handheld device that you hold in your hand, which has a thin metal strip inside that makes a distinctive clicking sound whenever you push down on the button. You can find a good-quality clicker at most pet supply stores; an added bonus is they are quite inexpensive. If you prefer, you can download an app on your phone that duplicates the clicking sound.

In positive reinforcement, we use a short marker word(s) to show our approval. The clicking sound is faster than you can say "Good Boy," and much more effective than training with treats and healthier for your dog's waist-line. The clicker allows you to communicate effectively to your dog, by showing him exactly what you liked about his behavior and solves the problem of having to dig a treat out of your pocket in time to reward him.

In clicker training, the clicking sound, over time will replace your "Yes" of approval. When you ask your Poochon to sit down, the instant his butt hits the ground, you activate the clicker, followed with a reward as quickly as possible.

How to use a clicker:

1. Choose a calm area for training without any distractions, such as your backyard. Choose a moment when your dog is hungry, preferably before meals, to start clicker training. Be sure to have a handful of treats in your hand or pocket.

2. First, you need to teach your Poochon the meaning of a click. Click the device in your hand and immediately give your dog a treat and praise him generously.
3. Repeat this activity five to ten times each day until he associates the sound with the yummy reward.
4. Start using the clicker in training sessions to reinforce good behavior. Once your Poochon learns the positive effects of the clicking sound, the noise starts acting as a reward in itself.
5. Once you and your dog have mastered clicker training, you can move on to more complicated commands and even tricks.

A clicker creates an unmistakable, distinct sound that only occurs when you are actually holding the clicker and training your dog.

An advantage to using a clicker over a marker word is that the click doesn't convey any emotional tone such as happiness or sadness, as it is just a click.Neutral sounds such as the clicker eliminate the stress or confusion your Poochon may feel around trying to figure out your mood.

How to use the clicker for basic and advanced commands:

1. At the exact moment your Poochon completes the desired action, press the clicker. Then, reward him with a treat and with praise.
2. Be aware that if you are not able to click at the exact moment your dog performed the new behavior, he might not associate the new action with the treat.
3. For more complicated commands or tricks, you can click and reward for small steps towards the desired behavior. For example, if you are teaching him to fetch the ball and bring it back to you, click for fetching then again when your Poochon brings the ball back.

The clicker does not replace yummy treats but over time you will be able to slowly wean your dog off those high-calorie treats, as the sound of the click becomes the reward. You will still need to give him an occasional treat, otherwise, the clicker will lose its effectiveness.

If you have an older Poochon with teeth or weight issues, a healthier option to doggy treats is to give him a few pieces of unseasoned cooked chicken or turkey breast during the clicker training sessions. Remember, your dog lives in the moment, so when you click the clicker, immediately give him a treat, so he can learn to associate the clicking sound with a treat.

Test your Poochon when he is playing or distracted by clicking the clicker. If he immediately stops whatever he is doing and looks at you, then you know he is ready to start being weaned off treats. If your pooch does not acknowledge the sound, then you know you need to spend extra time training with the click-treat combination.

One of the most common mistakes with clicker training is that pet owners forget to give their dog verbal praise. Your Poochon will associate the clicker sound with a yummy reward, but he still needs your verbal approval. Never ignore your pup's need for love and affection from you. Remember your Poochon thrives on your praise and smile of approval.

Tips for successful clicker training:

- Try using a clicker with a wristband as it will stay tethered to you and prevents you from accidently dropping it.
- Place the treats in a baggie. You only have two hands and a baggie allows you to keep the treats close at hand yet still hands free.
- Keep all of your clicker-training sessions short and sweet. Poochons learn better in bursts of five to seven minutes than in long thirty-minute sessions.
- The clicker is not a remote control to cue your Poochon into doing something. The clicker only marks the moment your dog does something worth rewarding, not the other way around.
- Keep the clicker in a safe place, out of reach of mischievous children who will think it is a toy.

Physical Exercise

Being a good puppy parent means providing your pup with daily physical activity. The benefits of regularly exercising your Poochon are endless. Regular physical activity helps your Poochon to sleep better at night. Just a slight case of sleep deprivation for your dog can cause all sorts of behavioral issues. You will notice your pup's overall mood will improve with daily exercise.

Another reason to regularly exercise your Poochon is that it helps keep his weight down. In the United States, more than fifty percent of dogs are considered to be overweight or obese. Like people, excess weight leads to a long list of health problems. Exercise also improves blood circulation, which decreases the risk of cardiovascular diseases.

A few health benefits for dogs derived from regular physical activity:

- Maintains and builds muscle mass, which can reduce risk of injury.
- Helps to prevent canine diabetes and certain cancers.

- Decreases the risk of urinary tract infections, as exercise stimulates frequent urination.
- Helps to reduce the risk of arthritis.
- May increase your Poochon's lifespan. However, other aspects can negatively affect this, such as diet, dental care and living conditions.

There are other benefits derived from providing your Poochon with a regular exercise regime. For example, just sticking to a walking schedule can combat many common behavioral problems.

Exercise gives your Poochon an opportunity to burn off his energy in a healthy way. If you exercise your dog randomly and without any structure, you will not see any improvement. However, if you follow a strict exercise schedule, you can eliminate or reduce the following:

- **Aggression** - Poochons can develop the canine equivalent of cabin fever. Regular exercise helps your pooch to release his tension, meaning he will be much calmer when back home.
- **Destructive behavior** - If your Poochon does not have a regular energy release, he will focus his energy by chewing on your furniture, digging, scratching and other destructive behaviors.
- **Barking** - One of the main reasons for excessive barking is related to a lack of exercise and can easily be eliminated by a few rounds of fetch in the backyard each day.

Tips on how to exercise your Poochon

Taking your Poochon for a walk around the block is a great way to begin, but there are countless opportunities to give him more exercise and have fun at the same time. If you have any questions about whether or not your particular type of exercise is safe for your puppy, check with your veterinarian.

Walking - Your Poochon lives for going for walks but remember to stop and let him sniff out his surroundings. Walking is an excellent form of physical activity but exploring his surroundings can also be quite stimulating and exciting.

Swimming - Poochons love water and swimming is a fantastic exercise, especially for an older dog who is suffering from joint problems as it is a low-impact exercise. If you are taking your Poochon out on a canoe or a boat, do not forget to put a life-jacket designed for dogs on him.

Hiking - Your Poochon loves the great outdoors just as much as you do. Take your pooch along with you on your next adventure to explore a new park or trails in your city. Always keep an eye on your Poochon for fatigue and make sure your dog has access to cold water and shade anytime he is exercising.

Fetch – Fetch is never boring for your Poochon in fact he could play for hours. Switch up the ball with Frisbees or your pup's prized chew toy to keep him on his toes. Exercise of this nature will release endorphins which will have an overall calming effect on your pup's behavior.

Games – Inclement weather may dampen your outdoor plans but there are plenty of games to help your Poochon burn off excess steam. For example, hide-and-seek or chase gets your pup moving. Tug-of-war can build muscle and a special bond with you. Poochons love a good game of tug.

Exercise Requirements for your Poochon

As mentioned above, exercise plays a vital role in your Poochon's overall health and may even extend his lifespan. However, providing your pooch with adequate exercise goes beyond taking him out for an occasional walk or two.

All Poochons are considered to be moderate to high energy dogs and require at least thirty to sixty minutes of exercise each day to keep them healthy and to keep boredom at bay.

Puppies – Puppies need several bouts of short exercise sessions throughout the day but excessive exercise for puppies may be detrimental to their growth. Over-exercise refers to repetitive actions, such as walking briskly or running for an extended period of time, not typical playing in the yard or romping around the house. A good rule of thumb is five minutes per day for each month of age.

Adults – An adult Poochon is considered to be in his prime from one year old to seven years old, and requires, on average, sixty minutes split up into two thirty-minutes or three twenty-minutes sessions a day. There will be days when the weather is bad, so you will need to offer other indoor alternatives.

Seniors – Do not make the mistake of assuming your elderly Poochon does not need exercise. Unless your pooch has serious health conditions that prevent him from exercising, you will want to continue with his daily walks. Regular exercise can relieve joint pain and maintain muscle mass. Plus, being out in the fresh air will put a little pep in your old pup's step.

Health exceptions – Some health conditions, such as patellar luxation (trick knee), may require strict bed rest while recovering to reduce swelling and manage pain. However, after that, a veterinarian will suggest doing strengthening exercises, such as walking uphill to build muscles around the knee.

Pregnancy – In general, pregnant Poochons should be taken for daily walks and exercised as normal, except for the last week of pregnancy. Regular exercise will help the pregnant dog stay in shape, which will help in her labor and delivery. Exercise can gradually resume two to three weeks after giving birth.

Photo Courtesy of Caitlin Murphy

Tips to Keep Your Poochon Mentally Stimulated

Just like humans, dogs may get bored of their same old everyday routine. Actually, one of the main factors behind behavioral issues is due to boredom. Bored dogs develop destructive behavior and may start chewing on furniture, digging up the garden or trying to escape from the yard.

Here are some creative ways to stimulate your Poochon so he does not get bored and start misbehaving.

Teach him a new trick

Engaging your Poochon in training sessions does not only teach him a new command or trick but it provides him with a mental challenge. Once you move past the basic commands, then move on to more advanced commands. Even older dogs will benefit from training sessions, often helping them become less anxious and calmer around other dogs.

Play together

Purchase a board game such as canine cards, puzzle or dominos, which allows you to place one or two pieces of kibble or yummy treat in some of the game parts. Give your Poochon one of the many toys with a hidden treat and let him try to figure out how to work it out. Another option is to play hide-and-seek or treasure hunt. Your pup will love the challenge and it will be a wonderful opportunity to bond together.

Run errands with your Poochon

Even a quick errand to the mailbox, grocery store, or friend's house will leave your Poochon feeling quite stimulated. (Remember, you should never leave your dog alone in the car even if it's for a few minutes.) Your Poochon will absorb the new sounds, scents and situations. By the time you get home, your pup will fall right asleep, even though it was not physically taxing.

Give him a task to do

Dogs were originally bred for hunting, herding, and retrieving. In the case of your Poochon, he is part Poodle, who was originally bred to retrieve birds from marshes. A hearty game of fetch or Frisbee will leave your Poochon feeling satisfied. He will not tire of bringing you back the ball, over and over again like it is his job.

Socialize your dog

Every time your pooch meets a new person or fellow canine, he is being exposed to new butts to sniff, new faces and new sights. Taking your

Poochon to a d og park gives him an excellent opportunity to engage his senses. Or take your dog for a walk down main street; he will love all the attention from everyone wanting to stop and pet him.

Switch up your pup's toy collection

Nobody wants to play with the same old toy day after day. Give your Poochon a toy to play with and when he becomes bored of it, replace it with another one. Keep all of his toys in a box and rotate them out. Your pup will love it when you switch up his toys, just as if he is getting a brand-new toy.

CHAPTER 9

Basic Commands

Training your Poochon will teach him basic good manners, such as politely greeting guests when they arrive, walking properly on the leash, and coming when called. By teaching your dog these basic commands, you are setting him up for a happy and safe life. Plus, a well-mannered dog is loved by all!

Many of the misunderstandings between dogs and humans are related to a communication gap. However, obedience training takes time; think of it as a marathon and not a short sprint. Some commands your pooch may learn in a day or two, and others may take a few weeks to master.

Photo Courtesy of Adele Hughes

Benefits of Proper Training

Your Poochon will bring you years of companionship, joy and a sense of pride. When a dog is constantly disobedient or exhibits behavioral issues, it can be a source of stress for both you and your dog. Training your dog is your responsibility - not just for your dog's best interests but for your own peace of mind as well.

> **HELPFUL TIP**
> **Intelligence**
>
> Poochons are considered an intelligent and fast-learning breed just like their parent breeds! To prevent bad behavior due to boredom, it's important to make sure that these dogs get at least 20 to 40 minutes of exercise each day. This breed can also be prone to nipping if frightened, so be sure to focus on positive reinforcement while training.

Your Poochon's behavior reflects directly on you as his owner. No matter your dog's age or temperament, he can benefit from a little extra instruction.

Here are five reasons to why you need to train your Poochon:

- **Training benefits both you and your Poochon** - When you train your dog, he is not the only one reaping the benefits. Regular training sessions with your pooch helps you to understand your dog's needs and personality, making you an even better owner.
- **Training keeps your Poochon safe** - The more easily you can control your Poochon by using basic commands, the better you can protect him when unrestrained. A dog who bolts when he is off the leash is likely to run in front of a car and get hit, or even escape out the front door before you are ready to leave.
- **Training helps your Poochon to be more sociable** - Obedience training teaches your Poochon his limits, boundaries and how to behave in social situations. As a result, other people and dogs will enjoy being around your dog.
- **Training makes traveling a breeze** - Nobody enjoys being around a disobedient dog. A well-trained dog will obey your commands but also those of others. Training will make boarding easier, either at the kennel, a close friend's house or a relative's home.
- **Because you can teach an old dog new tricks** - Old dogs can learn new tricks. It is never too late to improve your Poochon's education. With a little extra patience, an older dog can learn just as well as younger dogs.

A well-behaved dog experiences less stress and, anxiety, interacts better with others, and over time will form a stronger bond with you. One of the best gifts you can give your dog is your time and energy to train him, which will make him a happier and healthier dog in the long run.

Photo Courtesy of Hannah Inman

Picking the right rewards/treats

The principle behind positive reinforcement is when your Poochon acts in a way to please you, then he is rewarded for his efforts. Rewards can be a variety of things, such as getting to play fetch with you, playing with his favorite chew toy, or getting scratched behind the ears. But for most types of obedience training, the best reward is an edible one – a scrumptious treat!

Picking the right treat to motivate and encourage your Poochon is essential. Enticing treats for dogs come in a wide assortment of flavors, sizes, textures, and shapes. But some training sessions require a more appetizing reward with a stronger scent, such as meat and cheese.

However, many treats your Poochon loves are often high in fats and sugars. These fats and sugars may be a hidden cause of weight gain, health issues, or even dental problems.

It can be easy to lose track of the amount of treats you hand out throughout the course of the day. Depending on your Poochon's activity level, a ten-pound dog may burn only three-hundred calories each day. If one medium-sized doggy biscuit contains roughly thirty to fifty calories, just two or three of these can become an overindulgence.

- Choose treats which are especially formulated for dogs, as they are designed to please their palate without causing tummy upset.
- Choose treats that have added nutrients or benefit your dog's teeth.
- Keep track of the calories you give your dog each day in treats and subtract these from his total daily caloric intake.
- Try to keep treats under 10 percent of your dog's daily intake.

Due to the wide variety of treats available, try to make wise choices. Be sure to read the ingredient label and check for fat content. Ask your veterinarian for recommendations about the best type of treats to use for rewards for your Poochon. Here are some useful tips to help you choose the best reward for different training situations:

Small-sized treats – Smaller-sized treats can quickly be gobbled up, making them ideal for keeping your Poochon motivated and attentive during training sessions. If your dog spends too long chewing a treat between repetitions, cut the treat in half.

Soft and smelly treats – Soft, smelly treats will be your Poochon's favorite treats. These treats are better suited for training your dog to do more complex commands, such as "Roll over"or "leave it." Or perhaps you have stepped up your pup's training sessions to a public area with more distractions, this type of treat will keep him motivated.

Chewy treats – Some training sessions will need the treat to last a little longer, such as crate training or learning to stay still on the couch. For these occasions, a chewy treat is ideal as it keeps your dog distracted for a longer period of time.

Switch it up – Dogs can become bored with the same old treat. For training, mix a bunch of different treats together in a baggie to keep your Poochon intrigued, especially if he is struggling to learn a new command.

Basic Commands

Your Poochon will love learning these basic commands with you, as it means spending time with you and having your undivided attention. It is fundamental to start teaching your dog these commands as soon as possible because it will help him grow into a well-behaved dog who is a pleasure to be around.

If your Poochon is adopted, he most likely knows most of these basic commands already but may need to take a refresher course. Just be more patient with your older dog because he may be dealing with mobility issues. Training your dog, no matter his age is an excellent way to spend time together and have fun!

Your Poochon is a fast learner and he is eager to please you, so use that to your advantage. With kind and gentle guidance, you should be able to teach your pup to sit, come, stay, etc. in a few weeks' time.

Keep in mind while training your Poochon:

- Training sessions should be short and sweet. Your pup's attention span is short and you want to make learning fun, so plan on each session to be five to ten minutes.
- Avoid training your dog when you are grumpy, upset or irritable, as your Poochon will only pick up on your foul mood.
- End each training session on a positive note by repeating a command he has already mastered.
- Start training your Poochon in an enclosed area with zero distractions; as he masters different commands, move to a new environment, such as a park, or a spot along your walking route.
- Never verbally or physically hurt your Poochon. Obedience training is based on positive reinforcement by using rewards, such as treats, praise, and affection.

All of the following commands can be combined with clicker training. Simply press the clicker whenever your dog successfully does the specified behavior then give him a treat.

Photo Courtesy of Jayne Dixon

As we noted earlier, keep commands simple. Say "Sit" instead of "Sit down here."

When training your Poochon, pay close attention to the tone of your voice. Never yell at your dog as he has exceptionally good ears and can hear you very well. A loud, angry voice is not going to teach him anything except the fact that you are upset. Patiently show your dog what you expect of him, speak in a soft, kind voice and praise him affectionately.

Sit

Teaching your Poochon to sit is one of the most important commands, thus making it the best choice to start with. Once your dog knows this command, he will be much calmer and easier to control. Plus, the sit command is the foundation for other commands, such as stay and come.

Here is how you teach your Poochon to sit:

1. Hold a treat near to your dog's nose.
2. Slowly move your hand upward, allowing his head to follow the treat, which will cause his bottom to lower to the ground.

3. Once your Poochon is in a sitting position, say "Sit," and give him the treat and affectionately praise him.

Repeat this sequence a few times a day until your Poochon has mastered it. Then start asking your dog to sit before dinnertime, going for walks, or any other situation you want to teach him to be calm.

Stay

The stay command is similar to the sit command and makes your dog easier to control in certain situations. This command is handy for moments when you need your pooch to stay out of the way as you clean your house or if you do not want him to overwhelm your houseguests.

Here is how to teach your Poochon to stay:

1. Tell your Poochon to sit.
2. Once he is sitting, then open the palm of your hand in front of you and say, "Stay."
3. Take a few steps backwards. Reward him with a yummy treat and affection if he stays sitting.
4. Gradually increase the number of steps you take backwards each time before rewarding your dog.
5. Always reward your Poochon for staying still, even if it is only for a few seconds.

This command teaches your dog self-control, so do not be discouraged if it takes a little longer than you thought. Most dogs, especially Poochons prefer to be on the move, exploring their surroundings instead of simply sitting still and waiting.

Down

This can be a challenging command to teach your Poochon, as it requires him to get into a submissive posture. Be sure to keep the training sessions for this command fun, upbeat, and positive. Also, never forget to praise and reward your dog once he successfully follows through on the command.

Here is how to teach your Poochon to get in the down position:

1. Tell your dog to sit.
2. Use a particularly delicious-smelling treat and hold it out in front of you in a closed fist.
3. Place your closed fist in front of your Poochon's snout. When he sniffs it, slowly move your hand towards the floor, so he follows the treat.

4. Slide your hand along the ground in a vertical line towards you, to encourage his head to follow.
5. Once he is in the down position or lying down, say "Down," give him the treat in your hand and generously praise him.

You will need to practice this command daily until your dog has mastered it. If your pooch tries to lunge towards your hand say a firm "No," and take your hand away. Never push him into a down position; instead, encourage him every step of the way until he figures out how to please you.

Come

This command is a godsend for times when you lose grip on the leash or accidentally leave the door open. This command is quite easy to teach and will keep your Poochon out of trouble.

Here is how to teach your Poochon to come:

1. Put a leash and collar on your Poochon.
2. Get down to your dog's level and say, "Come," while gently tugging on the leash.
3. When your pup comes to you, be sure to reward him with treats and affection.

Once your Poochon has mastered coming to you with the leash on, then attempt the same sequence without the leash, in a safe enclosed space.

Off

Off can easily become confused with "Down." The Off command is used to teach your Poochon not to jump on people or to climb on certain furniture. The goal is for your dog to keep all four paws on the ground.

Here is how to teach your Poochon OFF:

1. When your dog jumps up, say a firm, "Off," and point to the floor. Once he is standing with all four paws on the ground, reward his good behavior.
2. If you found your Poochon on the couch, and he is not allowed to be there, say a firm "Off," and encourage him to come to you. When he comes, reward him with a treat and praise.

Another way to avoid this bad behavior is by simply ignoring it. When he jumps up on you, turn around and act like you are leaving. Wait a few seconds and then try again. Reward your dog when he does not jump up on you.

Leave it

This command can keep your Poochon safe when his curiosity gets the better of him such as when he smells something on the ground that may be potentially dangerous for his health, if he eats it. The goal of this command is to teach your dog that he will get something even yummier if he ignores the other item.

Here is how to teach your Poochon to leave it:

1. Place a treat in each of your hands.
2. Open one of your hands with the treat inside and say "Leave it."
3. Close your fist again; ignore any behaviors such as licking, sniffing, pawing or barking at your hand to get the treat.
4. Once he stops, give him the treat from the other hand.
5. Repeat until your Poochon moves away from the fist when you say "Leave it."
6. Next, give your Poochon the treat in the other hand only when he looks up at you and away from the closed fist.

It is vital to maintain constant eye contact with your Poochon during this command session. Make sure in your second hand you always have a yummy, smellier treat and in the other hand, just an ordinary piece of kibble.

How to Introduce the Leash and Collar

Some Poochons are quick to embrace their collar and leash, while others tend to shy away from them.

Whether you live in an urban or rural setting, your Poochon is going to need to learn to use a collar and leash. Often the breeder will introduce your Poochon to a collar when he is only a few weeks old. The first thing you need to do is make sure you have all of the right equipment for training your pooch to walk on a leash.

Below is just a short overview of the different types of collars and leashes available, and their uses:

Standard collar – This is your basic collar often used to place your dog's ID tags, etc. Poochons are expert escape artists and they will easily slip their head out of a standard collar.

Muzzle harness – This type of collar is not popular and its general idea is to keep your dog from following his nose, instead focusing on you. Often, this type of harness is used for training sessions for show dogs.

Back harness – This style of harness is great for smaller breeds such as your Poochon. This style of collar prevents their airway from being damaged from pulling on the leash. Also, it prevents your four-pawed friend from sliding out of his collar.

Martingale collar – A collar option for dogs who have the tendency to pull on the leash. It is a double-looped collar, which tightens when your dog pulls on the leash. There is no need to worry about choking, as it only tightens enough to be uncomfortable.

Standard leash – This classic leash, can come in a variety of styles and lengths. It can be a rope style or a flat band.

Retractable leash – A retractable leash has a coiled-up compartment, allowing you to let out as much length as desired or lock it so your Poochon cannot go any further.

Photo Courtesy of Sophie Clarke

The following steps will help you train your pup to use a collar and a leash:

Step 1. Go to a neutral space, such as your living room or backyard, and let him sniff the collar. Put the collar on your dog when he is distracted. Once he is used to the collar, attach the leash and let him run around with it behind him while in the house. Just keep an eye on him to make sure he doesn't get the leash caught on anything and possibly hurt himself.

Step 2. Take your Poochon for a walk around the block or to a neighbor's house. This will allow your pooch to get used to the leash and collar while in a safe environment. If your Poochon walks without pulling, give him praise and treats.

Step 3. Now you are ready for a real walk. When you start walking, if your Poochon pulls or tugs on the leash, do not painfully pull back on the leash. Just stop walking and say "No." When your dog stops pulling on the leash, give him a reward and affection.

Advanced Commands

Now that you have mastered all of the basics, you can consider moving on to more advanced commands. These tricks will keep your Poochon active, fit, and mentally stimulated. Plus, they will strengthen the bond you share with your four-pawed pal.

Remember that obedience training is an ongoing process. You will never completely be finished. You will need to keep working with your Poochon throughout his lifetime. For example, people who learn a second language at a young age but later stop speaking and using the language, may eventually forget much of it as they grow older. The same goes for your Poochon. Do regular practice sessions to reinforce commands and tricks he has already learned, so they can stay fresh in his mind. Plus, it is an excellent way to bond and spend time with your dog.

Look

Teach your Poochon to pay attention to you or something in particular.

1. Hold a treat between your thumb and pointer finger, so your Poochon can see it.
2. Bring the hand holding the treat up to your nose and hold it there.
3. Say the command, "Look."
4. Hold the treat there for a few seconds then give him praise and the treat.

Repeat the sequence until he completely masters the command and only give him the treat when he is directly looking at you. This command lays the foundation for more complex commands such as "fetch" or "drop it."

No

This might seem like a basic command, but dogs tend to quickly forget it because they hear it so often in day-today conversations. You will need to constantly reinforce this simple yet crucial command. This command will teach your Poochon to stop whatever he is doing when he hears the "No" command and look at you.

1. Ask your Poochon to sit.
2. Place one of his all-time favorite treats in front of him on the ground so he can see but it is still out of reach.
3. When he lunges forward to grab the treat say, "No." Raise your hand in a stop sign. Your hand will be the barrier between the treat and your dog. Do not raise your voice or yell at your dog.
4. You need to pay constant attention while practicing this command, as your pooch will try to sneak in a few treats.

The goal of this command is to teach your Poochon to look at you when you say, "No" and not at the treat. He should look to you for permission to eat the treat. Once your dog looks to you, then pick up the treat and give it to him. Repeat this command until he has mastered it and can wait a minute or two when he hears the "No" command.

Roll Over

This is a difficult command to teach because it is physically difficult to guide your dog through the movements without having to help him roll over.

1. Tell your dog to go into the down position.
2. Hold a treat between your thumb and pointer finger, so he can easily see it. Place it close to his nose.
3. Do a backwards circle with the treat in front of his gaze, causing him to follow the treat. The movement should result in him flopping over on his side while trying to roll over.

The first few times you practice this, you might have to help your Poochon roll over, so he can follow the treat. Say the command, "Roll over," as he is in the process of rolling and give him the reward at the end.

CHAPTER 10

Traveling

According to a recent survey, more than 68% of US households own a pet dog and about 37% of pet owners regularly travel with their dogs every year.

When making travel decisions, choose the safest and most comfortable option for your Poochon. For instance, unless you will be able to spend the majority of your time with your pooch, he will most likely be happier left at home than tagging along with you on your journey. But if you have decided to bring your pet along, follow the suggestions and tips below and have a safe, stress-free trip.

Photo Courtesy of Krystal Williams

Preparing Your Poochon for Travel

Whether your Poochon is a seasoned traveler, or you are planning your first big trip together, there are several things you can do beforehand to help make the trip less stressful for both you and your furry friend. Avoid travel drama by preparing your pup for travel as soon as possible.

- **Food** – Be sure to pack enough dog food for the duration of the entire trip, as switching your dog's food may cause him to have an upset tummy. If you are planning on traveling for a longer period of time, research ahead of time whether your Poochon's regular dog food is available in your final destination.
- **Water** – Throw in a bottle or two of clean drinking water to keep your dog hydrated throughout the journey. Never allow your dog to drink water from an unfamiliar source such as a creek, puddle or pond.
- **Food and water dishes** – Do not forget to bring your pup's food and water dishes along. Be sure to place them in an area where you can easily reach them, throughout the trip. If you are tight on space, look for a set of pop-up food dishes.
- **Crate or carrier** – Depending on your method of travel, you might need either a hard-cover crate or a soft-cover carrier. Make sure to choose a comfortable traveling case, as it will most likely be used as his personal bedroom when you reach the final destination. How to choose an appropriate crate is discussed in the following pages.
- **Toys** – Be sure to bring along a few of your Poochon's favorite toys for the journey, as this will keep him distracted during long-haul trips and also help to relieve stress.
- **Blankets and doggy beds** – A nice, fluffy blanket will keep your Poochon warm during the journey, plus the familiar scent will keep him calm. If you have space in your luggage, bring along his doggy bed so your dog can use it at the final destination.
- **Collar, leash and ID tags** – Be sure to place your dog's collar and ID tags on him before leaving the house and do not remove them until you return home. If your Poochon is an adventure-seeker, he may suddenly escape to explore his new surroundings, so you may want to invest in a GPS-dog tracker tag.
- **Cleaning supplies** – Traveling with dogs can get messy. Be prepared by bringing along potty pads, baby wipes, paper towels, disposable garbage bags and, of course, a pet friendly stain remover.

- **Medications** – If your Poochon is taking any type of medicine or supplements, make sure you have enough for the duration of your trip.
- **Health and vaccination certificates** – Do not forget to bring along your Poochon's medical information when traveling, in case of an emergency.

Traveling by Car

Whether you are taking your Poochon on a short trip or a long journey, you will want to ensure your pup is comfortable and safe.

Avoid the temptation to let your Poochon sit in the front seat or roam freely about the vehicle while in movement. If you have a car accident due to being distracted by your dog, you could be held accountable. Even worse, you or your pooch or other parties may be seriously injured.

Do

Secure your Poochon inside of a hard-cover crate that has been anchored to the vehicle by using a seatbelt or other secure means or placed on the floor.

Bring along plenty of clean drinking water to keep you pooch hydrated, even more so during the warmer summer months.

Give your dog plenty of rest stops, not only for your Poochon to relieve himself but also so he can stretch his legs and drink some water.

If you have the air conditioner on or a window open, make sure it is not directly blowing on your Poochon. If the window is open, make sure your dog cannot stick his head out or accidentally jump out.

If your pooch suffers from motion sickness, ask your vet to prescribe a mild medication and follow the vet's instructions.

Make your Poochon feel at home inside of his crate by bringing along some familiar items such as his blanket, chew toys, etc.

Bring along a human buddy. Whenever possible, share the driving and dog caretaking duties with a friend or family member. You will be able to use the facilities or grab a quick bite to eat knowing someone you trust is keeping a watchful eye on your Poochon.

Don't

Never transport your Poochon in the back of an open pickup truck.

Do not allow your dog to sit in the front seat and hang his head out of the vehicle while in movement. He could be injured by particles of debris or get sick from breathing cold air forced into his lungs.

Never leave your Poochon alone inside of a hot car. It only takes a few minutes for your dog to become overheated. This may cause irreversible organ damage or even death.

Do not feed your Poochon at least two hours prior to traveling, in order to prevent motion sickness.

A year-round hazard is leaving your Poochon unattended in your car. Any time you leave him alone inside the car, you are making an unspoken invitation to pet thieves.

Photo Courtesy of Ella Worley

HELPFUL TIP
Poochon Carry-On?

Depending on the airline, you may be able to take your dog onto the plane as a "carry-on" item. Typically, you will need to make sure that your dog can comfortably fit into a kennel that will be able to fit underneath the seat in front of you. Soft-structured kennels are ideal for this kind of travel. For best results, look for a carrier that is designed specifically for airline travel. Different airlines have different regulations, so be sure to check with your carrier before making plans to fly with your Poochon.

If your Poochon is wary about getting into the car, let him explore the vehicle on his own terms with the doors open and the car turned off. Then turn the car on so your dog can get accustomed to the sound of the motor running. Do not forget to praise your Poochon for his good behavior.

Once your Poochon seems comfortable to be inside the car with the motor running, place him inside his crate and take him for a short spin around the neighborhood. Be sure someone is sitting beside his crate in the back seat. Make sure the final destination is somewhere fun and memorable for your dog, such as the park, beach or even your backyard for a game of fetch.

Choosing the Right Crate for Long Distance Car Travel

Whether your Poochon loves long road trips or quivers at the very thought of getting into the car, you will want to make the journey as comfortable and pleasant for him as possible. Dog travel crates are designed to provide a safe, enclosed place for your Pochon to travel in comfort. These crates differ from your Poochon's home crate, as they come with extra security features such as fasteners to keep the crate secure while traveling.

Here are the factors to consider when choosing a travel crate for your Poochon:

Size – The crate should be big enough for your Poochon to sit, stand, lie down, and turn around in, but small enough to keep him secure. A general rule of thumb is that travel crates should be no more than six inches longer than your pooch. A bigger crate may give your dog more space to move about it, but this also means he may involuntarily slide around inside of the crate while the vehicle is in motion.

Soft vs. hard-cover – As mentioned earlier, a soft carrier may be more comfortable for your Poochon. However, for car travel, a hard-crate provides your dog with more protection if you get into an accident. Another advantage to hard-cover crates is that they are easier to clean up if your dog has an accident or gets carsick.

Harness - Due to new state laws, many car crates come with a built-in harness which allows the crate to be securely fastened to the seatbelt for extra stability. By fastening the crate to the seat, you are creating a more secure ride for your Poochon as the crate will not slide around on sharp corners or fly forward if you come to a sudden stop.

Visibility – Poochons are very curious by nature and love to observe their surroundings. Choose a crate that will give him an unhindered view and lots of fresh air. If your dog is nervous of car travel, then the more visibility, the better.

Traveling by Plane

Airlines are not only cramming people onto flights nowadays; they are also accommodating a growing number of dogs who are frequent flyers. For first-timers, bringing your Poochon along is definitely more expensive and complicated than flying solo, but it is possible with a little extra research ahead of time.

Generally, veterinarians and breeders do not recommend flying with your pet unless absolutely necessary. Ideally, dogs should not fly unless their owner is permanently moving to a new location or taking a long trip of two to three weeks minimum. This is because flying can be extremely stressful for your Poochon. Air travel removes your pooch from his comfortable home and familiar surroundings, forcing him into a strange environment with loud noises, bright lights, changes in air pressure and cabin temperature, and to make matters worse, few opportunities to use the bathroom.

Cargo or carry-on?

Where your Poochon will be allowed to spend his time during the flight will depend on his size. Rules vary from airline to airline. Typically, your dog will be allowed to fly in the cabin, as a carry-on, if he is small enough to fit in a carrier under the seat in front of you. Most airlines have a weight limit of twenty pounds for dogs flying in the cabin, though there are some exceptions. Any larger than that, and your dog will usually have to travel in the cargo hold, along with the luggage and freight.

Every year, hundreds of thousands of dogs fly in the cargo without incident, however, there are many unknown variables that you have no control over once you hand your Poochon off to the airline personnel.

Airlines do their best to make your dog comfortable in the cargo hold. However, baggage handlers are often just trying to get the plane loaded or unloaded ontime. They are not paid to give your dog extra attention inside of the kennel. Unfortunately, many pet owners have horror stories of their pets being injured, becoming seriously ill, getting lost, or even dying after flying in the cargo hold. So, if your Poochon is too big to fit under your seat in the cabin, seriously consider if the risks are worth it.

Photo Courtesy of Adele Hughes

How much does it cost?

Typically, it will cost approximately $125 each way to fly with your Poochon in the cabin, but it can vary by airline. The cost of shipping your dog in the cargo hold is relatively cheaper. It depends on the travelling distance, as well as the combined weight of your dog and his crate. The majority of airlines will provide you access to an online calculator to estimate the cost.

Research, research and research some more

Airlines have a long list of rules and guidelines for traveling with your dog, and they are constantly changing. It is important to read through them thoroughly before traveling so your Poochon is not turned away before boarding the plane. If you can, a few days before flying, phone the airline company to double check that you have all the required documents for traveling with your Poochon.

When planning your flight, look for a non-stop flight with no transfers. Avoid traveling with your Poochon during holiday seasons when airports are busy, and flights are packed. This is wise so as to minimize the risk of any unexpected changes or cancellations.

If your Poochon has no option but to travel in the cargo hold, be mindful of the weather at your final destination. If you are traveling somewhere cooler, choose flights in the middle of the day when the temperature is not as cold. If you are travelling somewhere warmer, opt for flights later in the evening or early mornings before the temperatures rise. Keep in mind, most airlines will not let your pet travel in the cargo hold if the temperatures are too extreme at the final destination.

The majority of airlines allow only a certain number of dogs each flight, so always call the airline and make sure they have space for both you and your Poochon. Always make reservations for you and your dog at the same time to avoid unwanted last-minute surprises at the airport.

Consider your destination

If you are planning on traveling internationally, or even to some U.S. states such as Hawaii or Puerto Rico, be sure to check into local animal transportation regulations before even purchasing your ticket. Many destinations have a complicated process and lengthy quarantine periods, which may mean you will be separated from your Poochon for part or most of your trip.

Before traveling, research the departing and destination airport so you know exactly where any pet-relief areas are located inside the airport. If you have flight transfers, your Poochon will thank you for letting him relieve himself and stretch his legs. Consult the terminal, so once your flight lands, you will know exactly where to head with your dog.

Consult with your vet

Before any flight, be sure to consult with your veterinarian about food, water and medication. The American Veterinary Medical Association does not recommend sedating your pet prior to flying. There are health risks with sedating your dog, and certain airlines prohibit sedating pets without a note from your dog's veterinarian. However, you can ask your vet for his opinion as he is familiar with your Poochon.

If your Poochon is slightly overweight, your vet can formulate a weight loss plan to help him lose those extra pounds before the big journey. This is important, as obese dogs are at a higher risk of having their airways collapse while traveling.

Many airlines require that your Poochon have a clean bill of health. Your veterinarian can issue a health certificate stating your dog is healthy enough to fly and is up-to-date on his vaccinations. If the duration of your trip is longer than the certificate's validity, then you will need to get another certificate from a veterinarian while on vacation to meet the requirements of your Poochon's return flight.

At the airport

Plan on arriving at the airport with plenty of extra time so you are not stressed or feel rushed.

If your Poochon is traveling in the cargo hold, most airlines require you arrive at least three hours before domestic flights and at least five hours before international flights. You may have to take your Poochon to a separate cargo drop-off section in the terminal, so review your departure and arrival airport maps ahead of time to avoid confusion.

If your Poochon is traveling with you in the cabin, you can go directly to the passenger check-in desk, where the agent will request to see your dog's health certification and proof of immunizations.

Once you pay the pet carry-on fee, you should head directly to security. Deal with your personal items such as computer, jackets, shoes, etc. before tending to your dog. Remove your Poochon from his carrier case and carry him through security, while his carrier goes through the X-ray machine. To speed things up, do not forget to remove your dog's harness or collar so it does not set off the metal detector.

If you checked your Poochon into the cargo hold, be sure to paste a current picture of your dog on the crate along with his name. Also, you can tape a bag of food to the outside of the crate in case of a long delay. Be sure to have a current picture of your Poochon on your phone and picture of his crate, in case the airline accidentally misplaces your dog, which is not likely to happen, but it is better to be prepared than sorry.

In the cabin

Once inside the aircraft, your Poochon has to stay inside of his carrier for the entire duration of the flight. You are not permitted to take him out of his carrier to cuddle him or place his carrier on the seat beside you.

Hydrate, Hydrate, Hydrate – Keeping your Poochon well-hydrated during the flight is vital for his well-being. Many carriers come with an attachable water dispenser, which will keep your Poochon hydrated during the flight. However, before traveling, you will need to get your Poochon used to drinking water inside of the carrier case or crate.

If your dog is hesitant to drink from the water bottle, then entice him by filling it with lukewarm chicken broth. Water dispensers have a ball inside of the cap that rolls around when touched, releasing water. You might have to encourage your Poochon by rolling the ball around and releasing the irresistible scent of chicken broth. Reward him when he drinks from the bottle, and slowly wean him off the chicken broth by replacing it with water.

Treats – Just as babies cannot pop their ears during the change of pressurization upon take-off and landing, your Poochon can't either. To avoid this, give your pup a few pieces of a jerky treat to chew on to avoid any ear issues during the flight. Be careful not to give him too much as he could get air sick.

Prepare for potty accidents - To prevent spillage from an unavoidable accident in-flight, place a disposable potty pad on the bottom of the crate. Plus, be sure to bring along a few gallon Ziplock bags in case your Poochon goes potty mid-flight so you can easily clean up and dispose of the soiled pads.

Upon arrival

If your Poochon travelled in the cargo hold, pick up your checked luggage upon arrival and go straight to your airline's specified location for cargo. Airlines often state that dogs will be available thirty minutes after the flight's arrival. If your dog is not picked up in four hours from arrival, the airline will hand the dog over to a veterinarian or boarding facility at your expense.

Whether your Poochon flew in the cabin or the cargo hold, take him immediately for a walk, so he can stretch his legs and relieve himself in a designated relief area for pets either inside or outside of the terminal. Even though the journey may seem complicated, you both will breathe a sigh of relief when you arrive at your final destination together.

Choosing the Right Crate for Air Travel

Yes, we are back to talking about crates and carriers, and with good reason. Whereas a hard-sided crate is recommended for the cargo-hold, the best type of crate for traveling in the cabin is a soft-sided carrier as it can easily fit under the seat in front of you. Hard-cover crates may be quite cumbersome to fit under the seat in front of you. Plus, hard-cover crates are heavier to carry around inside of the airport.

The specified carrier dimensions to fit under the seat in front of you differ from airline to airline. Just because the crate or carrier you plan to purchase says "airline approved" does not necessarily mean it is suitable to be used on al aircrafts.

When choosing a carrier for air travel, look for one that is slightly larger than necessary to give your Poochon a little extra breathing space to stretch out. If you are planning on taking a cross-country or international flight, look for a carrier that expands to give him a little extra space during the long flight.

Familiarize your Poochon with his carrier or crate well in advance to the actual flight. If possible, take your dog to the airport's departure area several times so he becomes more comfortable with this noisy, strange place.

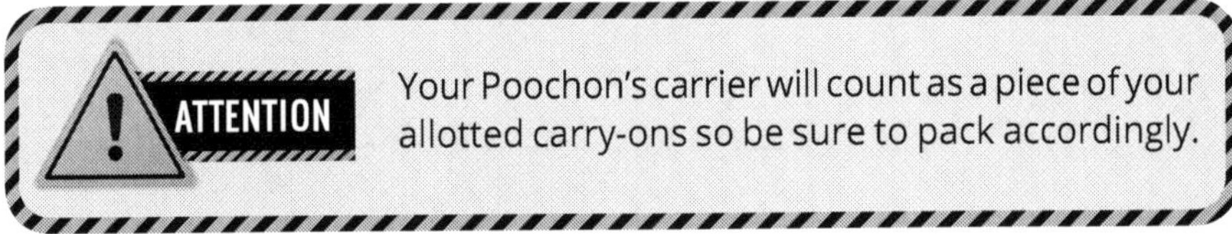

Lodging Away from Home

Hotel Stays

Talk directly with the hotel – Book directly with the hotel over the phone. This way you will be able to ask any specific questions regarding the hotel's policies and fees for overnight pet guests. Ask the following questions:

- If there is a pet fee, is the fee per night a flat rate or for the entire stay?
- Do they require a damage deposit?
- Is the entire hotel pet-friendly or only a designated floor? If they say the latter, ask whether the restaurants or lobby area are pet-friendly?
- Can you leave your dog in the hotel room alone or does he need to be supervised? If so, how long does the hotel's policy allow your dog to be left unattended?

- Do they offer dog sitters or dog walkers? If so, what are the costs and availability for your stay?
- Are there any charges associated with damages from your pet?

The majority of hotels charge a nominal fee for dogs, often $25 to $50 is a standard price per night. Many major hotel chains or boutique hotels offer discounts for pets during their off-season.

Take into consideration your Poochon's behavior – You will never really know how your Poochon will act when traveling until you try it but taking into consideration his behavior at home will help you determine how he will act at the hotel. For example, if your pooch tends to bark at people walking past the window, then request a hotel room on a higher floor. Or if your Poochon gets nervous on elevator rides, request a room on the lower floor so you can just walk up the stairs.

If you have to leave your pup alone in the room, put the television on so he will not get nervous or excited by hearing people walking and talking in the hallways. If you are unsure how your pup will act, you can always plan a short-one night stay at a local pet-friendly hotel. Or if your Poochon loves the sound of his own voice, maybe consider staying at a pet-friendly rental property.

Have a back-up plan if you cannot leave your dog alone – If the hotel policy is that you cannot leave your dog alone in the room, make sure you have a backup plan. Most hotels offer additional services, such as a dog sitter or a dog walker for hire. Another option is to take your Poochon to a day spa or the groomer for the day.

If the hotel lets you leave your dog alone in the room, always give the front desk staff a heads up and give them your cell-phone number in case of any noise complaints or other issues. Also, place the DO NOT DISTURB sign on the door, to prevent a housekeeper from accidentally frightening your pup.

Choose the right pet-friendly hotel – Just because a hotel lets your dog stay as a guest, it does not necessarily mean it is pet-friendly. Many boutique hotels provide amenities to cater to their four-pawed guests, such as a dog bed, some yummy treats and food dishes for an additional fee. A few chain hotels even invite their furry guests to their nightly, complimentary wine reception.

Research pet-friendly restaurants and activities - If you cannot leave your pooch alone in the hotel room, you are going to want to find restaurants or activities that are pet-friendly. The majority of hotels will provide you with a list of nearby restaurants that allow pets. Often, if a hotel is pet-friendly, at least a part of the lobby or onsite restaurant will accommodate your pooch.

Look for fun activities to do with your Poochon that are dog-friendly, such as a walking tour of the city or spending the day exploring a dog beach or park. Many galleries, zoos, wineries, and vineyards are pet-friendly if your dog is leashed at all times and under your supervision.

Tips for a quiet hotel stay

Nobody wants to be that person... the one whose dog barks in the hotel room. It can be heartbreaking to realize that your Poochon was upset at being left alone in a strange place and embarrassing knowing you are responsible for disturbing the other guests' peace. Plus, it may cause you an expensive inconvenience if the hotel asks you to leave.

If you must leave your furry friend alone in a hotel room, even if it is a short period of time, these steps will help you and your dog avoid any problems:

- Do not leave your Poochon alone until he has become acclimated to the new space. Take the time to establish in your dog's mind that this room is his "new home."
- Try doing a few practices by leaving the room for a few minutes then coming back inside. This will help your dog understand that if you leave, you will be returning promptly.
- Keep your time away as short as possible.
- If available, upgrade your room to a suite. By having two separate living spaces, you can place your dog's crate in the furthermost corner from the hallway. This will act as a buffer, giving your pooch some space from those strange noises outside of his door.
- Tired dogs make less ruckus. Be sure to take your Poochon for a long walk with plenty of opportunities to relieve himself outside.
- Pack something extra special to keep him distracted while you are out and about such as a toy stuffed with a delicious treat. If your pup's mouth is busy, he will be less likely to bark.
- Help your Poochon relax by playing classical music and leave it playing when you go out to cover any hallway noises that may trigger barking.

When staying with friends or family

Visiting family and friends is already a challenge and adding your Pochon into the mix simply makes the whole situation a little more interesting. No matter where you are planning on staying, your pup needs to learn to be a gracious house guest. The sooner you can start teaching your dog proper pet-etiquette, the better.

The preliminary step, of course, is to ask permission to bring along your furry friend. Not everyone wants a dog as a house guest. Even dog lovers appreciate an advance warning, as it allows them to puppy-proof their home, such as putting away those porcelain collectible figurines on display. The strain of an unwelcome dog can permanently damage relationships. So, even if your Poochon was welcome in the past, never assume he is welcome again – ask first!

Another factor to take into consideration is if the host or other house guests may be allergic to dogs, or maybe there are small children present who are uncomfortable around rambunctious pups, such as your Poochon.

Training is a critical aspect of whether your Poochon will make a gracious house guest. The better trained your pooch is, the more welcome both of you will be as guests. Ask yourself if your Poochon has mastered the basic commands such as: sit, stay, and come. It may seem like a long list but there are key elements for your dog to be a charming guest.

Photo Courtesy of Ralph Makison

If your Poochon is prone to bad behavior such as destructive chewing, non-stop barking or house-soiling, it is unfair to expect your co-host to welcome your dog into their house.

Regular exercise, chew toys and dog puzzles can keep behavioral issues at bay. Bring your Poochon's crate so he has a place of his own when he needs a little down time. Be quick in cleaning up, especially if the mess involves your dog's hair on Granny's black jacket or slopping drinking water on the floor from his dish. Ask your hosts, where is an appropriate spot in their backyard, for your dog to relieve himself and be quick to clean up his messes.

If things do not work out as planned, have a contingency plan, such as a pet-friendly hotel nearby or even a reputable boarding kennel. No matter how things go, send a thank-you card to express your gratitude and if necessary, to apologize.

Boarding Kenneling vs. Dog Sitters

Unfortunately, there will be occasions when you cannot take your Poochon with you, meaning you will have to choose between boarding your dog in a kennel or hiring a dog-sitter to watch over him while you are out of town. There is no ideal solution, but taking into consideration your dog's age, temperament, and needs, will make the decision a little less worrisome.

Boarding Kennels

Boarding kennels are basically a pet hotel for your Poochon.

Your Poochon's stay at the boarding kennel includes grooming, attention, and daily exercise. Depending on the kennel you choose, they will offer a variety of packages and prices to cater to your pup's individual requirements. If you are considering this option, here are a few advantages and disadvantages:

Advantages to boarding kennels:

- Boarding kennels provide a secure environment with experienced, dog-loving employees who will constantly monitor your Poochon to prevent any incidents.
- Often the kennel hosts other friendly dogs, giving your Poochon plenty of fun opportunities to socialize with other dogs.
- Your pup will follow a strict schedule during his stay, which will reduce his stress levels. From your Poochon's first day there, he will be fed and exercised according to a schedule.

Often there is a veterinarian on-site or on-call if there are any emergencies. This option is especially helpful if your Poochon has chronic health problems, as he will receive constant monitoring.

Disadvantages to boarding kennels:

With all the different dogs staying at the kennel, things can get quite chaotic and noisy at times, which can be stressful for sensitive dogs. If your Poochon tends to get nervous in a new environment or around other dogs, maybe boarding your dog might not be the best option.

Although the kennel staff do their best to keep everything in check, certain situations can get out of control. There is a small risk factor if your Poochon accidentally gets into a scuffle with another dog.

Depending on the size of the boarding facility, staff could mix up food, toys or blankets between different dogs. Often, this does not cause too many problems, except perhaps an upset tummy.

Keep in mind, if you leave your Poochon at a boarding kennel, he will spend the majority of his time inside of his kennel.

All boarding kennels require that their doggy guests' vaccinations and immunizations be up-to-date. No matter the age of your dog, he is required to have received his Rabies and Bordetella (kennel cough) vaccine at least seven days prior to your dog's planned arrival date.

Bordetella is an airborne upper respiratory infection. There are almost sixty different strains, and the current vaccine only protects against fourteen. There is no way to fully protect your Poochon from kennel cough as it is highly contagious. For this very reason, it is of utmost importance to search for a boarding kennel that prides itself on regularly sanitizing everything your pup might come into contact with, such as playground areas, daycare areas, toys, food and water dishes, etc.

Boarding kennels have the right to refuse the admittance to any dog if the pet owner lacks adequate proof of a dog's vaccinations or if the dog has serious health conditions or displays aggressive behavior.

Dog Sitters

A dog sitter is someone who cares for your dog in your home while you are temporarily absent. Typically, the dog sitter will stay in your house or drop by several times a day while you are away, allowing your Poochon to feel safe and secure in his own territory. Having a dog sitter stay overnight is the ideal solution if your pooch suffers from separation anxiety or you prefer not to leave him alone at night.

Advantages to a dog sitter:

➕ While you are away, your Poochon is in the comfort of his own home. There is no need to worry about your pooch being exposed to a new environment, people or other animals.

➕ The risk of accidents or injury is reduced because a single person is devoted to caring for your Poochon.

➕ Your dog sitter will carefully follow all of your care instructions for your dog and perhaps even water your plants, if you ask them to. If you have a younger pup, you can teach the dog sitter how to work on your dog's obedience training and basic commands.

➕ A dog sitter will directly communicate with you if there are any problems, etc. The direct line of communication will give you peace of mind, so you can focus on your holiday.

Disadvantages to a dog sitter:

➖ A dog sitter needs to come into your house and it is imperative you and your Poochon trust her or him. If your pooch is protective of his home or does not react well to new people, perhaps a dog sitter is not the best option.

➖ Having a dog sitter stay in your home requires extra preparation, such as readying the guest bedroom where they will stay.

➖ During holiday season, it can be almost impossible to find a reliable dog sitter. Be sure to book ahead of time.

➖ If you hired a dog sitter to drop by a few times a day and there's bad weather, they might not be able to get to your house regularly.

Pick the right sitter – Try to choose someone whose energy level and personality matches that of your dog. For example, leaving your rambunctious puppy with an elderly relative is a recipe for disaster. Make sure you feel comfortable with the dog sitter and that they understand your Poochon's individual needs.

Finding a professional and responsible dog sitter should not be taken lightly, after all they will be responsible for your pup's welfare and you are entrusting them with the keys to your house. Here are a few suggestions to help you find a reputable dog sitter to care for your dog:

- **Ask your veterinarian** – If your Poochon is elderly or has health issues, finding a dog sitter with a good rapport with your vet will give you peace of mind, especially if there is a medical emergency.
- **Word of mouth** – Anyone can look good on paper, but a qualified, reputable dog sitter will come recommended by a close friend or a relative.

- **Ask for references** – Any reputable dog sitter will be able to provide you with a list of regular clients who would be more than willing to verify their professionalism.
- **Look for a certified dog sitter** – There are two nationwide agencies that train and certify dog sitters: Pet Sitters International (PSI) and The National Association of Professional Pet Sitters (NAPPS). Be sure to check out their webpages to locate a certified dog sitter in your locality, plus you can check out their reviews from previous clients.

Location – Ideally, you want someone who can stay at your house to maintain your Poochon's regular routine and schedule. This involves keeping your dog on the same walking, feeding, and sleeping routine as when you are at home. If you must change your dog's routine, get him used to the changes a few weeks ahead of time, to prevent separation anxiety or other issues.

If you plan on leaving your dog at a friend's house while you are away, you might want to get him familiar with a new location a few times before actually leaving your dog there for an extended stay.

Details – Just as parents leave a checklist for a babysitter, you can make a checklist for your dog sitter. Include important information such as the vet's phone number and address, any medications your dog needs to take while you are away, allergies, feeding schedule, the closest twenty-four-hour emergency veterinary clinic, and any behavioral problems.

Share with the dog sitter any house rules for your Poochon. For example, whether he is allowed on the furniture and how often he gets a treat - basically, any information you feel will keep your pup feeling happy, satisfied and secure while you are away.

Relax – Now take a deep breath and relax! You have taken all of the necessary steps to ensure that your Poochon has a pleasant experience while you're away, so enjoy your mini vacation.

You will have to take into consideration your Poochon's personality and needs to make the best choice while you are out of town. Carefully consider the advantages and disadvantages of each option and weigh them against your dog's requirements in order to make the ideal decision. If you cannot decide which is the best choice for your canine friend, you can always try a short stay at a boarding kennel and another with a dog sitter before your actual planned trip to see how you dog reacts.

CHAPTER 11

Nutrition

A nutritious and balanced diet is essential to keep your dog healthy. Every Poochon is different. Some dogs love to eat, others are picky eaters or have a sensitive stomach, and there are dogs with dietary sensitivities. Deciding on what to feed your Poochon is a very personal choice. In this chapter, you will learn the building blocks to provide for all of your dog's nutritional needs and more.

Importance of a Wholesome Diet

Your Poochon's diet will have a direct impact on his health and happiness. Just like humans, dogs require essential nutrients to develop properly and stay healthy. The wrong diet can lead to a life of health issues and obesity. The right diet will keep your dog slim, healthy and in tip-top shape.

The old saying, "You are what you eat" applies to your Poochon as much as yourself. Dog food made with high-quality ingredients equals a better-quality of life, resulting in fewer infections, digestive issues, skin conditions, etc. The impact of a wholesome diet does not end there as it can directly impact your dog's personality and behavior.

Here are a few examples of how your dog's diet may directly impact his overall health, mood and personality:

Unbalanced diet – A diet lacking in nutrients can cause your Poochon to suffer from frequent urinary infections that cause him to become irritable due to pain and discomfort. A well-balanced diet that provides all of the nutrients your dog needs will be both emotionally and physically healthy.

Lack of food – If your Poochon is not receiving enough calories throughout the day, he will be hungry and may even resort to destructive behaviors, such as chewing, scavenging, or eating his feces. If a dog receives inadequate daily nutrients, he may develop a condition called "pica" which causes him to eat non-food items, such as dirt and plants.

Quality of ingredients – Make sure the dog food you choose is designed for your Poochon's life stage, size, lifestyle, etc. For example, puppy food contains a higher level of the fatty acid DHA, which increases their mental alertness. On the other hand, senior dog food is enriched with antioxidants to help fight off diseases. Studies have shown that senior dogs who have always received a high-quality dog food suffered from fewer behavior changes common with cognitive decline.

A well-balanced diet will promote stable blood sugar levels throughout the day, which will directly affect your Poochon's serotonin levels. Serotonin is considered to be the happy hormone and not only improves your dog's mood but also his concentration, behavior, and training response. Another

Photo Courtesy of Victoria Lumby

advantage to a wholesome diet is your Poochon's immune system will be in excellent condition.

When choosing a dog food brand, take into consideration your Poochon's age, size, weight, medical history, and lifestyle. Ask your veterinarian for recommendations as to what brand of dog food is best suited for your dog's optimal health.

When a dog gets sick, we often assume it is due to exposure to something external, and we never think it could be caused from the food we are feeding him.

Here are some common health issues related to your Poochon's diet:

- **Heart disease** – Dogs often have issues with heart disease, especially if their diet is not well-balanced. Increased levels of sodium are one of the main factors of heart disease in dogs. Since high-quality commercial dog foods are low in sodium, the main source of sodium is coming from those table scraps you are slipping your dog under the table.
- **Diabetes** – Overweight dogs tend to develop diabetes as they age. There is no known cure for diabetes. A dog with diabetes will require daily insulin shots, a special diet and extra medical attention. The best and only prevention is to keep your Poochon on a healthy diet and give him an active lifestyle. Avoid dog food that contains starchy fillers and sugar, which offer little to no nutritional value and will spike your dog's blood sugar level.
- **Obesity** – Obese dogs are prone to arthritis, diabetes, breathing issues, high blood pressure, and cancer. Decreased life expectancy is linked to obesity in dogs. Your Poochon does not need too many calories each day. Be sure to follow the instructions on the food bag for his weight, size and age.
- **Pancreatitis** – Pancreatitis is caused by a diet high in fats. Consult with your vet to see if your dog's current dietary fat intake may be increasing his risk of pancreatitis.

Food allergies and sensitivities

It is important to take into consideration how a particular food affects your Poochon. If your dog's energy level is normal for his age, if his coat and skin are healthy, if his stools are brown and well formed, and if he appears to be healthy, then his food is doing its job.

However, if your Poochon has diarrhea, skin issues, or an extremely itchy coat, your dog may have a food sensitivity. In this case, the best thing to do is to discuss the issue with your veterinarian. He will be able to help you create a feeding plan that works best for your dog's health.

Food sensitivities can be managed and often disappear over time. On the other hand, allergies are a more serious food problem. If your Poochon has a food allergy, often it presents as an immediate immunological response, such as anaphylactic shock. In this case, you should take your pooch to the nearest veterinarian clinic immediately. A less severe reaction may present itself by facial swelling, hives or itchiness. If you suspect your Poochon has a food allergy, it is vital that you talk to your vet to identify the cause.

HELPFUL TIP
Allergies

Poochons may be more prone to skin allergies than some other breeds. While triggers for these allergies can range from pollen to tick bites to household cleaners, some pet owners find that diet plays a role in maintaining a dog's healthy coat. Omega-3 fatty acids may help reduce inflammation if your dog suffers from skin allergies. Always talk to your vet before making dietary changes. Too much Omega-3 supplementation can cause your dog to have an upset stomach.

Human Foods to Avoid

Slipping your Poochon a morsel or two under the table may be tempting, but it can cause your dog some serious health issues or even be fatal. You might be surprised at some of the foods your furry friend needs to avoid at all costs!

Alcohol – Even the tiniest amount of any type of alcohol can be fatal for your Poochon. Alcohol causes dogs to have coordination problems, vomiting, diarrhea, breathing issues, and even death.

Avocado – All dogs are allergic to persin which is found in high quantities in avocados. Persin is not only found in the flesh of the avocado but also in the leaves, peel, bark of the tree, seed, etc. If you happen to have an avocado tree in your backyard, be sure to keep your dog away from it at all times.

Bones or fat trimmings – It might seem like second nature to give your pooch a bone to chew on, but smaller dogs, like Poochons, can easily choke on them, or the bone may splinter and become lodged in his throat or cut up his digestive system. Pieces of grease or fat can cause your Poochon to develop pancreatitis.

Caffeine – All types of caffeine are fatal for your Poochon, including cocoa, energy drinks, Guarana, tea, caffeinated carbonated beverages, and soda. If your dog accidentally consumed a product with caffeine, go immediately to the nearest veterinarian office.

Chocolate – Dark, white, and milk chocolate are deadly for dogs. Even the smallest morsel causes diarrhea, vomiting, cardiac failure, seizures, and even death.

Dairy products – Dairy products such as milk, whipped cream and ice cream can cause your dog to experience digestive discomfort and diarrhea. Many dogs who are lactose intolerant have extremely itchy skin. The majority of dogs can tolerate cheese and yogurt due to the natural digestive enzymes and probiotics.

Garlic and onions – Keep all types of garlic and onions far away from your pooch, including fresh, dry, powdered, dehydrated or cooked. Even the smallest pinch can cause your Poochon's blood count to drop, causing him to become anemic.

Grapes or raisins – Grapes and raisins seem the perfect bite-sized treat for your dog, but a few can cause kidney failure. If you think your Poochon may have consumed some grapes or raisins, call your veterinarian if you notice any sluggish behavior or severe vomiting.

Macadamia nuts – Eating just three macadamia nuts can cause your Poochon to become seriously ill. Eating chocolate-covered macadamia nuts will only intensify the symptoms which will eventually lead to death. Macadamia nuts cause vomiting, muscle tremors, fever and loss of muscle control.

Pitted fruits – Fruits such as peaches, persimmons, cherries and plums have pits or seeds that can get lodged in your dog's intestines, causing a blockage. Some pits, such as from a plum or a peach, contain cyanide, which is fatal if consumed.

Raw eggs – Raw eggs are a source of bacteria, such as Salmonella or E. coli. Avoid feeding your Poochon raw or undercooked eggs or any type of raw animal products – fish, beef, pork or chicken.

Raw yeast dough – Before baking, yeast dough needs to rise. If your Poochon eats some raw dough, it will continue to rise inside his stomach, stretching out your dog's abdomen, causing extreme pain. The yeast can also cause alcohol poisoning.

Salt – A word of caution: Do not share your salted popcorn or pretzels with your furry friend.

Too much salt can cause sodium ion poisoning, vomiting, diarrhea, fever, or seizures, and may even be fatal if left untreated.

Xylitol – Xylitol is a common sweetener used in baked goods, toothpaste and diet products. It causes your dog's blood sugar levels to drop, which leads to liver failure.

If your Poochon got into the pantry and ate something he shouldn't have, call your local vet immediately or call the Animal Poison Control Center (ASPCA) – (888) 426-4435.

It is not advisable to make a practice out of giving your Poochan leftovers, bits of meat or other scraps as he may begin to refuse to eat his normal food without them. Also, it can unbalance your dog's regular diet causing him to gain weight. Human foods can cause wind, which may not be a problem for your dog but it could be for you!

Photo Courtesy of Jen Swanson

After all that talk about harmful human foods for your pooch, you are probably wondering: "Is all human food bad for my dog?" Although you may use great self-control to keep your Poochon on his canine diet, sometimes you cannot resist the urge to slip him a piece of cheese.

Below is a short list of human foods that are safe for canine companions. Before giving your dog any foods that are not on this list, do some research to make sure they are safe for him. If your pup experiences any sort of reaction or allergy, immediately consult a veterinarian. Here are some of the best human food choices for your four-pawed furry friend.

Peanut butter – Peanut butter is a favorite treat for Poochons around the world. Also, it is an excellent source of protein, healthy fats, vitamin B, and niacin. Be sure to only use unsalted peanut butter. Make sure you are not using sugar-free or lite peanut butter, as it may contain artificial sweeteners such as xylitol.

Cooked chicken or turkey – Cooked chicken is a healthy source of protein and makes a great alternative to high-caloric treats used in obedience training. Plus, if you accidentally run out of dog food, it makes a healthy meal replacement.

Cheese – Cheese is an excellent snack for your pooch if he is not lactose intolerant. Choose low-fat varieties and do not overfeed, as most cheeses are high in fat and may cause constipation. Cottage cheese is typically a good option for Poochons.

Carrots – Carrots are a yummy low-calorie snack for your dog and are great for your dog's teeth. They are also high in fiber, beta-carotene and vitamins. You can feed your dog raw or cooked carrots, just be sure to cut them into small pieces to prevent him from accidentally choking on them.

Yogurt – Yogurt is high in calcium and protein, also its active probiotics can aid your dog's digestive system and improve his breath.

Salmon – Salmon is an excellent source of omega 3 fatty acids, which will help keep your Poochon's coat healthy and shiny and support his immune system. Try adding cooked salmon to your dog's kibble or slipping him some of your unwanted fish skins.

Pumpkin – Pumpkins are part of the squash family, all of which are excellent sources of fiber, beta carotene and vitamin A. Plus, pumpkin can keep your Poochon's GI tract moving and aid with digestive issues.

Eggs – A scrambled egg will give your Poochon's diet a protein boost. Eggs are remarkably high in protein, and a source of digestible riboflavin and selenium. Always thoroughly cook the eggs to avoid any risk of salmonella.

Green beans – Green beans are another healthy snack for your Poochon, as they are a source of protein, calcium, vitamin K, and iron. Raw and cooked green beans are filling and low in calories. Just remember to only serve them without salt or other seasonings.

Apple slices – Sliced apples are high in fiber, and vitamins and a healthy treat for your Poochon. Additionally, apple slices are known for cleaning dog's teeth and freshening their breath. Before giving your dog a few apple slices, make sure to remove the seeds and the core, as they can be a choking hazard.

Oatmeal – Cooked oatmeal is an excellent source of soluble fiber, which is especially beneficial to senior Poochons with bowel irregularity issues. It is a fantastic grain option for dogs allergic to wheat. Always cook oatmeal before serving to your pup and only use oatmeal that has no added sugar or additives.

If you decide to give your pooch a treat or two from your table, make sure it is not seasoned, fatty, salty, or raw. Certain fruits, such as thin slices of apples, bananas or watermelon all make yummy treats for your Poochon. Be sure to remove any seeds, peels or stems that could get stuck in your dog's digestive tract. Cooked, plain white rice or noodles with a piece of boiled chicken might be the best solution if your pooch has an upset tummy.

Commercial Dog Food

Commercial dog food has improved enormously over the last few years. In the past, there were only a few generic brands on the shelf, whereas today, you can choose from hundreds of different brands, which cater to different breeds, ages, and diets. However, with so many choices out there, it can be overwhelming narrowing down what type of dog food is best suited for your Poochon.

There are two main types of commercially prepared dog food: canned foods or dry kibble. Commercially produced fresh dog food will get an honorable mention as it is a newbie to the dog food aisle and is just starting to emerge.

Wet dog food

Wet dog food may be sold in cans, boxes or single-serving pouches, often consisting of 35% to 75% water depending on the quality. Be sure to look for the moisture content on the label. Wet foods contain a variety of meats such as beef, chicken, lamb, salmon, or venison.

One of the advantages to wet dog food is it is preferred by finicky eaters, by toothless dogs and for concealing medications. Another advantage is that wet foods are beneficial for dogs who dislike drinking water or are prone to urinary tract infections. Once the can or package is opened, however, it must be refrigerated to maintain its freshness, and most Poochons will not eat cold food. To solve this problem, you can warm up the meal portion before serving.

The packaging method uses a high-heat sterilization method, destroying many of the essential nutrients and vitamins. The sterilization and vacuum-sealing process ensure a longer shelf life without the need of using harmful chemicals. However, due to the processing method, wet foods are notorious for being void of nutrients. If you want your dog to get his daily nutritional requirements, you will need to give him a huge portion at each meal, which will eventually result in weight gain.

Some Poochon owners try to entice their fussy pooch to eat their meals by mixing in a small portion of wet food into their dry kibble. It is worth mentioning that wet foods have the highest cost per serving and cheaper brands of wet food are high in fillers, sugar, and fat.

Dry food

The vast majority of dogs throughout the United States are fed dry kibble. Kiddle's popularity is due to the convenience for feeding and cost (as with most things, the larger the bag, the better the savings). One of the main advantages to dry food is it acts like a toothbrush, helping to remove and prevent the build-up of plaque and tartar on your dog's teeth. In addition, it stays fresh longer than wet foods once the package has been opened.

The following is a list of different types of methods used to manufacture dry dog food:

Baked - The kibble is baked at a low temperature to prevent a loss of nutrients. Baked kibble often contains wheat gluten to bind the ingredients together and artificial preservatives to lengthen its shelf life.

Cold-pressed – This newbie on the dog food aisle is quickly gaining popularity with both pet owners and dogs alike. The process involves using fresh ingredients then grinding them together to form a coarse paste which is left to dry before pressing the excess moisture out of it. It is then baked a very low-heat to prevent nutrient loss.

Extrusion - This is one of the most popular methods for manufacturing doggy kibble. The method involves grinding all of the ingredients into a fine powder, then pressing that into kibble. The kibble is then cooked in huge steam/pressure cookers to kill off any bacteria, etc. After this, the kibble is placed into a high-heat convection oven to remove any excess moisture. The kibble's double exposure to extreme heat removes the majority of nutrients and vitamins.

Freeze dried – The fresh food is mixed together then ground into a coarse paste, formed into small pieces of kibble and placed inside a type of vacuum oven that removes all excess moisture. The process preserves the majority of the nutrients, making it one of the healthiest choices for your Poochon. Freeze-dried foods have a long shelf life without the need of harmful preservatives. Some freeze-dried foods may need to be re-hydrated with water before serving. This is one of the most expensive dry dog food options to purchase.

Fresh food - A newcomer in the dog food market, this is quickly gaining popularity as a convenient option to homemade dog food. Fresh dog food is made from fresh human-grade proteins, organic grains, and veggies. Many companies provide the option of using recyclable or reusable serving trays.

One of the main advantages to fresh dog food is the high-nutritional value due to the low level of processing required. On the other hand, since it does contain preservatives, fresh food has a maximum lifespan of seven to fourteen days and will need to be stored in the refrigerator. However, by freezing and unthawing food, many of the nutrients will be lost.

As you can see, there are a lot of factors to consider when choosing the best dog food for your Poochon. The different types of dog foods mentioned above, each have their own pros and cons. Choosing a dog food is ultimately a very personal decision and depends on your ethical values, budget, and personal preferences. Ultimately, the right dog food for your Poochon is one that meets his nutritional requirements and keeps him healthy and happy.

How to Read Dog Food Labels

If you have ever walked down the dog food aisle at your local pet supply store, you can confirm that there are hundreds of different brands all claiming to be the best option for your pooch. The dog food label is the best tool to use to help you make a choice, but often it can be difficult to understand.

Quick tip: Look past the attractive packaging and marketing, instead learn to read the ingredients.

General rule of thumb: If humans are not allowed to eat it, then you should not feed it to your dog either.

Ingredients do matter

Dog food labels are required to contain:

- Product brand name.
- Quantity displayed in terms of weight, liquid measure or count, depending on the formulation of the dog food.
- Ingredient listed in descending order by weight.
- Feeding instructions for your dog's age, activity level and weight.
- Nutritional statement backed up by research and testing to prove the food provides the required daily nutritional requirements.
- Manufacturer's name and address.
- Calorie statement and the life stages the food is appropriate for.

As mentioned above, the first ingredient listed on the label comprises the most weight. Continue reading to learn which ingredients to avoid and why they can harm your Poochon's health.

Artificial preservatives – Avoid dog foods that contain ethoxyquin, BHA and BHT on the ingredient list. The National Institute of Health has deemed BHA and BHT to be a carcinogen and unfit for human consumption. Ethoxyquin is linked to cancer, chronic immune diseases, and kidney failure in both humans and animals.

Corn and rice fillers – Corn and rice fillers are commonly used for fattening up animals, and the last thing your Poochon needs is a carbohydrate-rich diet. A low-protein diet is one of the main causes for obesity in smaller breeds, such as your Poochon. A diet high corn and rice can cause chronic digestive issues, such as bloating, gas and diarrhea.

Food coloring – Many dog food manufacturers add food coloring to their kibble and treats to make them look more appealing and appetizing. But, honestly, your Poochon is not concerned about the appearance or color of his food; he just cares about if it is tasty. Avoid dog foods that contain food dyes such as Blue 2, Red 40 or Yellow 5 because they are linked to causing allergies, hyperactivity, and cancer.

MSG – Monosodium glutamate (MSG) is a well-known flavor enhancer for Chinese food and dog food. MSG over-stimulates your dog's brain, causing him to produce a hormone called dopamine, making him become addicted to his food. Recent studies have shown when dogs regularly consume foods with MSG over time, they can develop brain damage, obesity, and behavioral issues.

Nondescriptive fats – Fat is essential for your Poochon's overall health. Many dog food manufacturers vaguely list animal fat as one of the ingredients, which often is fat derived from sick or rancid animals. Instead, choose a dog food that specifies the type of fat used, such as salmon fat instead of fish fat or coconut oil instead of vegetable oil, etc.

Propylene Glycol – Propylene glycol is a common ingredient for antifreeze and is extremely toxic for dogs. However, many dog food manufacturers add it to their product to reduce moisture from building up inside of the packaging, to prevent bacterial growth and to lengthen the product's life-span.

Rendered foods – Rendered meat is often listed as animal by-product meal, which is a mix of animal parts such as blood, brains, spleens, entails and internal organs. More than often, it includes discarded animals that were considered to be unfit for human consumption. The nutritional value of rendered meat is extremely low and is a source of salmonella and toxins.

Sugar – Many dog foods contain sugar to mask a bitter flavor and to improve texture. Once your Poochon is addicted to sugar, it is extremely difficult to switch him to a healthier, sugar-free alternative. Sugar additives to watch out for are cane sugar, beet pulp, corn syrup, sucrose, fructose-glucose, xylitol, molasses, and sorbitol.

Deciphering terms

Recently there are so many new trends in the dog food market, it makes it even more challenging to decipher the terms. Here are some terms that can be difficult to understand:

Organic – As of the moment this book went to print, the U.S. Department of Agriculture (USDA) was still developing official regulations regarding the labeling of organic foods for pets. In the meantime, dog foods that claim to be organic must meet the requirements established by USDA's National Organic Program, which means organic dog food has to meet the same standard of organic human food.

Organic dog food must contain no artificial sweeteners, preservatives and flavorings, and food colorings. Plus, meat and meat by-products used must be sourced from animals with no antibiotics or growth hormones. Generally speaking, dogs with sensitive tummies do better on an organic diet.

Note: "natural" dog food is not the same as "organic." The term, natural dog food, refers to the lack of artificial ingredients used in the product.

Grain-free – Recent studies by the FDA have discovered grain-free dog foods are related to canine dilated cardiomyopathy (CDC), which causes the dog's heart to enlarge and prevents the blood from circulating freely throughout the body. The FDA recommends pet owners avoid feeding their dog's grain-free foods. Dogs need a diet based on high-quality proteins, natural fats, vegetables, and whole grains to meet their dietary needs.

New proteins – New proteins does not mean fresh. The term refers to new meats in the dog food market, such as bison, kangaroo, rabbit, lamb and other exotic animals. At the moment, it is difficult to rate the benefits of this food due to a lack of research on the different nutrient profiles when compared with common proteins such as beef, chicken or fish.

Human-grade dog food – This is defined as legally edible and safe for human consumption. Human-grade dog food is tightly regulated by the FDA and the USDA. Also, the Association of American Feed Control Officials (AAFCO) require that human-grade dog food be manufactured, packaged, and held in accordance with federal regulations for manufacturing, packaging and holding human food.

Light, low-calorie, and low-fat – If labeled with one of these terms, dog food must have a significant reduction in fat or calories when compared to the brand's standard dog food. The AAFCO requires that any dog food label claiming to be light, low-calorie or low-fat must show the reduction on the label and name the product in comparison.

Foods to look for:

Finding a wholesome, healthy and delicious dog food for your Poochon may be a challenge but not impossible. When choosing a dog food for your dog, look for a variety of ingredients such as meat, veggies, grains and even fruits. Here are some good ingredients to look for on the ingredient list:

Meat – Your Poochon needs protein for a healthy body and immune system. Look for a commercial dog food made from human-grade meat, such as beef, chicken, salmon, rabbit, etc.

Whole-meat meal – Often meat meal is from by-products such as rendered meats, whereas whole-meat meal is a high source of protein and is simply a fancier way to say, "ground beef." However, the ingredient list should specify the type of whole meat meal used, such as chicken, beef, etc. Meat meal contains more protein, as it is ground up then dried to a ten percent moisture level, making the protein level at least 65% and at least 12% fat.

Carbohydrates and grains – Whole grains are an exceptional source of energy for your Poochon and they improve his digestion. Shy away from dog foods made from corn, soy or white rice; instead, look for higher quality ingredients, such as brown rice, whole oats, barley and peas. Of course, carbohydrates and grains should never be one of the first ingredients on the ingredient list.

Vegetables and fruits – Both provide essential nutrients, minerals, vitamins, fiber and antioxidants. For example, sweet potatoes are an excellent source of potassium, vitamin B and antioxidants. Unsweetened cranberries provide vitamin C, prevent urinary tract infections, and protect your pup's teeth from harmful bacteria.

Fats – Fats are necessary for your Poochon's overall health, proper cell function and digestion. Fats help your Poochon to absorb minerals and vitamins and keep his coat and teeth in tip-top shape. Look for dog foods that contain wholesome fats like Omega-3 and Omega-6 fatty acids, canola oil, salmon fat, olive, and coconut oils.

Pay attention to the product name, as it will give you a clue about the ingredients in the dog food you are considering. Most dog owners base their decision on a specific ingredient. Many brands will highlight that ingredient in the product's label.

Stay away from commercial dog foods that use the term "with," such as "with chicken"' or "with beef." Manufacturers are only required to use 3% of protein in the dog food. Avoid dog food whose labels include the wording "flavor," such as beef or chicken flavor, as it indicates it was made with an exceedingly small percentage of the actual product and mostly contains artificial flavoring.

Just because a dog food manufacturer claims to provide everything your Poochon needs for his optimum health, it does not necessarily mean the food is really healthy. Take the time to carefully read the ingredient list, and make a decision based on the ingredients, not based the attractive packaging.

Making Homemade Dog Food

Your Poochon is part of your family, which means you are willing to do just about anything for him – including making him homemade meals.

Many dog food recipes that are online fall short of the nutrients needed to keep your Poochon strong and healthy, such as iron, copper, calcium, and zinc. A recent study by the University of California, School of Veterinary Medicine tested more than 200 recipes written by respected veterinarians. Unfortunately, the researchers discovered more than 90% of the recipes lacked essential nutrients for canine health.

Making your Poochon home-cooked meals involves more than throwing a bunch of ingredients in the slow-cooker and hoping for the best. It involves careful planning to prepare a well-balanced and complete meal that

Photo Courtesy of Nikki Thelwell

meets all of your dog's nutritional needs. Always consult with your vet before switching your dog to a homemade diet.

Your Poochon's daily diet needs protein (animal meat, seafood, dairy, or eggs), fat (from meat or oil), and carbohydrates (grains and vegetables). He also needs calcium from dairy products or even egg shells, and essential fatty acids (oils, egg yolks, oatmeal, etc.). The following guidelines will help you create your own balanced, homemade dog food recipe:

Meat products – Protein should make up 50% to 65% of your Poochon's diet. As it is the main component, choose organic lean meats without skin and fat. Include in your dog's diet boneless chicken, beef and fish. Make sure the meat is cut into small pieces as it will facilitate chewing and digestion. Adding up to 5% beef liver into your preparation is a nutritious and tasty addition.

Eggs – Eggs are an excellent source of protein; however, smaller dogs such as your Poochon should only eat half of one whole egg per day.

Dairy – The majority of dogs can tolerate plain yogurt, cottage cheese and ricotta. If your pooch suffers from lactose intolerance, try substituting dairy products with goat milk. Avoid using other types of cheese as they tend to be high in cholesterol, fats and calories.

Starchy vegetables – Beans, peas, potatoes, squash, and sweet potatoes are all great sources of fiber for your Poochon. If your pooch is overweight, you will need to reduce the percentage of starchy vegetables in his dog food. Cook all grains, beans, and starchy vegetables to make them easier to digest.

Other vegetables – Leafy veggies are high in fiber and low in calories, plus they are full of wholesome nutrients for your pooch. Avoid using raw, cruciferous vegetables, such as broccoli and cauliflower, as they can cause digestive issues for your dog. Chop and blend the vegetables together before adding them to the meat mixture when cooking.

Fruit – Fruit supports your Poochon's digestive health and provides a long list of vitamins, nutrients and antioxidants. Apples, bananas, berries, and papaya are all excellent options. Avoid grapes and raisins as they cause kidney failure.

Grains – Whole grains such as quinoa, barley, brown rice, oatmeal and pasta are all an excellent source of fiber. All grains need to be well-cooked so they can be properly digested by your Poochon. Note: white rice has low nutritional value and should only be used to settle an upset tummy.

Supplements – Even the best recipe using the highest quality organic ingredients will still lack in certain nutrients such as calcium. Another reason to add supplements to your dog's homemade food is if you are freezing the food into daily portions, many nutrients are lost when food is frozen then thawed. Closely follow the instructions on the supplement packaging for your dog's weight, size, and age. If you have doubts, you can talk to a pet nutritionist.

Make sure the diet is working

After your Poochon has been enjoying home-cooked meals for two to three weeks, take him to the vet to make sure he is not gaining or losing too much weight. If your dog's weight changed slightly, check it again in a few weeks. Your vet will regularly check your dog's coat, skin, teeth, and body condition for any issues that might be related to his homemade diet.

A Basic Recipe for Homemade Dog Food

The following recipe is a healthy alternative to canned dog food, as it is loaded with iron from fresh protein and veggies. It can be stored in the fridge up to a week or frozen and reheated later. The recipe below is a basic guideline, which you can adapt to your Poochon's personal preferences.

Doggie Style Stew

Total: Makes four cups (32 fluid ounces)

- 1 pound of chicken or beef, without fat, skin or bones (cut into small pieces)
- 4 oz. of beef liver, chopped
- 1 medium, steamed sweet potato, chopped
- 1/2 cup of steamed green beans, chopped
- 1 cup of cooked quinoa or oatmeal
- 1 cup of spinach, blended with a cup of water
- 1 Tbsp. of fish oil or coconut oil

Directions

1. Sauté the meat and liver together in a large pot with the oil until thoroughly cooked.

2. Add the rest of the ingredients and leave to simmer on low heat for ten to fifteen minutes.
3. Let cool and serve.
4. Store the leftovers in the fridge for a maximum of five days.

As mentioned before, be sure to cook all animal products thoroughly to kill any harmful bacteria and cook all grains, starchy vegetables and beans to make them easier for your Poochon to digest. Before switching your dog to a homemade diet, be sure to discuss your dog's specific nutritional needs with your veterinarian. Remember that switching your dog's food to homemade from kibble is a slow process, so patience is essential.

Weight Monitoring

More than 60% of all dogs in the United States are considered to be overweight and nearly all of their owners are in denial! Obesity is one of the greatest threats for your dog's long-term health.

Dogs, like people, have a harder time getting around if they are overweight. Losing weight can be a challenge for dogs at any age, but even more so as they get older. Despite the challenges, weight loss for dogs of any age is worth the effort. Slender pups enjoy longer lives, fewer visible signs of aging, and less chance of developing canine arthritis.

Health problems that are more common in overweight dogs include: pancreatitis, diabetes, heart disease, joint pain, ruptured ligaments, hip dysplasia, compromised immune system, and different types of cancer. If you cannot feel your Poochon's ribs and shoulder blades, if his waist is not discernible (a tuck behind his ribs), or if there is a roll of fat at the base of his tail – then it is time to face the reality and put your pooch on a diet.

We, as a society, are so used to seeing overweight or obese dogs, we think a healthy weight for a dog means he is underweight. As long as your dog's hips and spine are not protruding, he's not too thin. If in doubt, ask your vet for his professional opinion.

Here are some weight loss tips for your Poochon:

Feed your dog more protein and less carbohydrates

When it comes to weight loss, the ratio of carbohydrates to fats and proteins matters more than calorie counting. Poochons thrive on a high-protein diet, as it builds lean muscle and improves mood and mental agility. If your Poochon is overweight, look for a dog food that is high in protein, low in carbs and moderate in healthy fats.

Avoid feeding your pooch a high-fiber diet

Fiber will not satisfy your dog and can interfere with nutrient absorption. Instead, look for dog foods that contain whole grains such as quinoa, whole oats, and brown rice as they are an excellent source of fiber and protein, yet low in carbohydrates.

Reduce your Poochon's portion size

Instead of making drastic changes, start slowly by cutting back your dog's meal portion size by 5%. Reduce every three weeks by 5% until you are giving your pooch the amount of food specified for him on the dog food package. This strategy prevents your Poochon from losing weight too fast then gaining it back. Slow, steady weight loss means long-term success.

Measure everything your Poochon eats

One of the reasons your Poochon is overweight is because you have been eyeballing his dog food. The only way to accurately measure your dog's food is either by using measuring cups or even better, by using an electronic scale to weigh every meal. This takes a lot of discipline on your part, but you will be surprised to find that you were often feeding your dog twice as much as required. You can find a small scale at an office or kitchen supply store or online.

Make your dog's weight loss a family project

Feeding your furry friend, a smaller portion will not help him lose weight if he is getting breakfast leftovers, an afternoon snack or a treat or two throughout the day. Discuss your dog's diet plan with the entire family and be sure they cooperate. Allot each family a certain number of training treats to give your Poochon each day and encourage everyone to focus on calorie-free treats and rewards such as playing fetch, games, or praise.

Rethink the treats you give your dog

Treats and rewards often have three to five calories and they can quickly add up in a training session. Instead of store-bought treats, try using pieces of cut up skinless chicken breast. Most dogs are more concerned about the number of treats they are receiving and do not notice the size of the actual treat, so cut up chewy treats into smaller pieces. Use raw baby carrots, zucchini slices or small slices of apple, banana or melon for a healthier treat.

CHAPTER 12
Grooming Your Poochon

How can you resist snuggling with your Poochon on the couch, especially when his coat is clean and soft? But what can you do if your Poochon is starting to look more like a Tramp and not at all like a Lady or a Gentleman?

Grooming involves so much more than giving your Poochon the occasional bath or taking him to a professional groomer. Even if you let a groomer handle the complicated stuff, your pooch still needs regular daily grooming to keep him squeaky clean, to reduce shedding, and most importantly, to keep him healthy.

Brushing

Maintaining your Poochon's coat is not for the faint of heart, as his long, silky coat needs to be brushed every day to keep it clean and tangle free. As mentioned in the first chapter of this book, Poochons are a low-shedding breed, which means loose, dead hair collects in his coat, unless it is brushed out daily, matting the hair very quickly.

Daily, you will need to brush your Poochon using a slicker brush. Once you have removed all of the tangles or mats, you can move on to brush him using a bristle brush. If matted hair is an issue, leave your household scissors in the drawer where they belong. One wrong movement by a nervous pooch could result in injuring you or your dog. The best way to remove a knot or mat is by using your fingers, some pet-friendly conditioner, a comb, and a whole lot of patience.

HELPFUL TIP
An Ounce of Prevention

Poochons are a popular breed partly because of their hypoallergenic coat, but this beautiful coat can be prone to matting if not properly cared for. Preventing mats is much more comfortable than removing them, especially because matted fur can irritate your dog's skin, so be sure to aim for almost daily brushing and regular haircuts. A pin brush is a great option for Poochons with curlier coats. Combine that with a slicker brush for optimal matting prevention.

Regularly brushing your dog for a few minutes at a time can accomplish a lot in terms

Photo Courtesy of Michelle Anahory

of keeping him clean, as it removes dirt, burrs, and grass. Get your dog accustomed to being brushed while he is standing, as a groomer would, instead of lying down. If you have a hard time remembering to brush your Poochon daily, place his brushes in a place where you will see them, such as beside your reading glasses or next to the television remote.

All dogs shed, and your Poochon is no exception. Excessive shedding can easily be prevented by providing your dog with a healthy diet, plenty of exercise, and fresh air. If you notice, while brushing your dog, that he is losing more hair than normal, the cause may be one of the following factors:

- Hot spots
- Sarcoptic mange
- Food-related allergies
- Parasites, such as fleas, lice or mites
- An immune disorder, such as adrenal or thyroid diseases
- Cancer
- Anxiety or stress
- Pregnancy or lactation
- A bacterial or fungal infection, such as ringworm

During tick season, you may need to check more than once a day for ticks. As you brush your Poochon, check for sores, rashes, or signs of infection, such as redness, swelling, skin inflammation, and tenderness. If you notice anything suspicious, consult with your veterinarian as soon as possible. The same is true if you notice any patches of dry, brittle skin that falls out easily.

While brushing your dog, if you notice any foreign objects lodged in his eyes, ears, skin, mouth or paw pads, do not attempt to remove them yourself – always consult with your veterinarian beforehand.

Bathing

Even if you keep your Poochon's hair trimmed and short, he will still need to be bathed every three to six weeks, sometimes even more often, to keep his coat clean, short and tangle free. As you will recall, your Poochon is half Poodle which means he loves to play in water, especially mud puddles, so during the raining months you may need to bath your pooch more frequently.

Do not spray your pooch with scents or perfumes. Dogs in general are far more sensitive to fragrance than humans and many products contain harmful ingredients that your dog may ingest when licking himself. Fragrances can result in respiratory problems. The best way to keep your Poochon looking and smelling his best is by regularly bathing him.

The following steps provide you with everything you need to know to give your Poochon a bath:

1. Before your Poochon's bath, take extra time to brush out any extra hair, debris or heavy dirt. Place your pup in a large basin or tub filled with approximately four to six inches of lukewarm water.

Photo Courtesy of Angela Marshall

2. Thoroughly wet your dog down using a large pitcher or spray hose. If using a spray nozzle, make sure the water is neither too hot nor too cold.
3. Avoid getting water or soap in your Poochon's eyes, nose, and ears. Use a damp washcloth to remove any dirt or debris around your pup's face.
4. Once your Poochon is completely wet, gently massage the pet-friendly shampoo into his coat. Start from the top of his head working your way down to his tail. Pay close attention to under his legs, as Poochon's tend to sweat under these areas. Dilute the dog-formulated shampoo in water, so it is easier to rinse out.
5. Rinse and repeat if needed. Hold your dog still to prevent him from shaking the excess water out.
6. Take your Poochon out of the tub or basin and dry him off using a large, fluffy towel.

When bathing your Poochon, never use human shampoo, as it contains fragrances that could irritate his skin. Instead, look for a high-quality shampoo that was formulated especially for dogs. Avoid using an inexpensive dog shampoo as they often are made with harsh ingredients.

Poochons are water dogs, so they can easily confuse bath time with playtime. Keep your pooch distracted by placing a float toy inside of the tub.

Nail Clipping

Unless your Poochon is running around all day long on hard surfaces that help keep his nails short, you will need to cut his nails once a week. A general rule of thumb, if you can hear your dog's nails clicking against the floor or his nails get snagged on the carpet, then it is time for a trim.

The majority of dogs are squeamish about having their nails trimmed, so do not expect it to be your favorite shared activity, no matter how many treats your pooch gets afterwards.

Getting your Poochon used to getting his nails clipped at a young age will take the pain out of this weekly ritual. While your dog is still a puppy, rub your hands up and down his legs, gently pressing down between his toes each time. Never forget to give your pooch a yummy treat followed by a big boisterous "Good boy!" After about two weeks of having his feet massaged, you can attempt clipping his nails. This method works especially well if your older dog is ticklish or wary about having his feet touched.

If you are unsure about how to finely cut your pup's nail, ask your veterinarian or groomer for a short demonstration on how to trim his toenails to the right length.

There are two different types of nail clippers – scissor-type or guillotine. Both styles come highly recommended, so choose the style you feel the most comfortable with. Another option is a nail grinder which sand the nails down, however, it makes a loud, grinding noise and the vibration can frighten you and your dog.

Before clipping your dog's nails, be sure to give him a vigorous workout to burn off energy then ask a family member to help you. There is no need to clip all of your dog's nails at once. If he becomes skittish, you can clip one paw at a time, with breaks in between.

How to clip your Poochon's nails:

1. Hold your Poochon's foot steadily but gently as you spread out each toe. Hold the nail clipper at a slight angle, snipping from the top to the bottom. Cut off the tip of the nail, avoid giving the nail a blunt edge, instead following the natural curvature of the nail.
2. Snip off the tip of the nail avoiding the quick. The quick is the darker colored circle inside of his nail, which is the blood vein that runs inside of the nail. If you accidentally cut the quick, you will have one very unhappy dog and a bloody mess.

Photo Courtesy of Joanne Daly

3. If you accidentally cut your Poochon's nail quick, you need to use a nail cauterizer, such as cornstarch or styptic powder, which you can apply with a Q-Tip. Be sure to have a moist washcloth on hand to clean up the mess. Cutting your dog's nail quick hurts and trust me – he will remember this unpleasant experience for a long time.
4. Once you have finished clipping your Poochon's nails, do not forget to generously praise your Poochon with yummy treats and a healthy scratch behind his ears.

If you are using a nail grinder to trim your Poochon's nails, follow the same method as specified above, and simply hold your pup's foot and grind a little off each nail. This is highly recommended if your Poochon has darker nails, as you will need to be extra careful because it is almost impossible to notice the nail quick.

Do not forget to trim your Poochon's dewclaws. Since as they do not touch the ground, they tend to grow longer and will eventually grow back into your dog's paw, which can be very painful and may cause health complications.

If your Poochon shows aggressive behavior while getting his nails trimmed or you have a hard time keeping your hands steady, feel free to ask the groomer to clip his nails for you.

Importance of Good Dental Care

Despite common belief that a dog's mouth is cleaner than humans, your pup can still develop dental issues such as tartar, plaque, and gingivitis. As if bad breath was not enough, these canine dental problems can actually lead to life-threatening infections. Not to mention dental extractions can range up to more than a thousand dollars.

Practicing good dental care will extend your Poochon's life. Unfortunately, your Poochon cannot brush his teeth on his own. Get your pooch used to having his teeth cleaned by gently massaging his gums for about twenty to thirty seconds daily for about two weeks. Once he is comfortable with you touching his gumline, do the same procedure daily but including his teeth for another two weeks.

How to brush your Poochon's teeth:

1. Place a pea-sized amount of the canine toothpaste on the tip of your finger, then let your dog smell it and taste it.
2. Gently massage the toothpaste onto his gums. This will allow him to get used to the texture and the flavor.

3. Use a double-headed canine tooth brush held at a forty-five-degree angle to clean below the gumline.
4. Work on one spot at a time, until your Poochon gets used to the feel of the toothbrush inside of his mouth.

Your pup may not be keen on getting his teeth brushed at first, but over time he will get used to it. Choose a time when he is more likely to sit still for the entire procedure, such as after a vigorous walk or a game of fetch outside.

Make sure you speak softly and soothingly throughout the entire process and do not forget to reward your dog with a yummy treat afterwards. Be cautious not to overdo it the first few times or if your pooch becomes agitated. Take your time and increase the length of each session slowly.

Older dogs can learn to be comfortable with getting their teeth brushed, but you can make things easier for yourself by starting early with your dog when he is still a puppy.

Do NOT use human toothpaste for your Poochon, as most contain fluoride which is extremely toxic for dogs. You can find a dog formulated toothpaste at your local pet supply store, often in different flavors such as beef, chicken, or salmon. There is also dog mouthwash that is diluted in water to kill bacteria and prevent plaque buildup. However, just as with toothpaste, never use human mouthwash on your dog.

If brushing your pup's teeth ends with tears, hurt feelings, or blood, there are still a few other choices you can make to improve his oral health. Dry kibble is better for your Poochon's teeth than soft or wet food, as soft food can become stuck between his teeth, causing tooth decay. Also, there are synthetic bones and chew toys that have been specifically designed to strengthen your dog's gums and teeth.

Routine dental cleanings

Despite your best efforts, you will never be able to give your Poochon a deep, thorough cleaning using a toothbrush. Even if your dog has healthy teeth, it is wise to have your veterinarian give him an annual cleaning to remove any plaque and tartar buildup, clean the gum line and polish his teeth.

Common Dental Issues in Poochons

No matter how often you brush your Poochon's teeth, you should inspect the inside of his mouth at least once a week. If you notice any of the following signs, take your dog to the vet as soon as possible:

- Bad breath
- Your dog is constantly pawing at his face or mouth.
- A change of eating or chewing habits.
- Depression
- Excessive drooling
- Red, swollen, painful or bleeding gums
- Bumps or growths inside of the gum line
- Yellowish tartar buildup along the gum line
- Discolored, missing or misaligned teeth

Treating serious dental issues can be costly, but leaving them unattended may be more costly to your Poochon's overall health in the long run. Dental care may be a hassle, but regular maintenance is a money saver in the long run and may even be a lifesaver. Letting your dog's teeth deteriorate leads to expensive and painful vet visits down the road. Many dogs will need to be given anesthesia to have their teeth and gums cleaned.

By being familiar with the following common mouth issues, you will be able to determine if it is time to take your Poochon to see a vet:

Gingivitis – Gingivitis is caused by an accumulation of plaque, bacteria and tartar around the gum. Signs are swollen, bleeding gums, and extremely bad breath. Fortunately, it can easily be cleared up with regular brushing.

Mouth tumors – Mouth tumors look like small bumps or lumps on your dog's gums. They can be extremely painful and irritating for your dog while eating or drinking water. Mouth tumors will need to be surgically removed by a vet.

Periodontal disease – This gum infection results in tooth loss and a high risk of the infection spreading throughout the body, causing all sorts of maladies. Watch out for bad breath, nasal discharge, mouth pain, lack of appetite, and loose teeth.

Proliferating gum disease – This occurs when your dog's gum-line is over his teeth, causing a gum infection. It can easily be treated with antibiotics.

Salivary cysts – These are fluid-filled blisters located under your dog's tongue or along the corners of his mouth. They will need to be professionally drained and cauterized.Often the saliva gland will need to be surgically removed.

Moral of the story: keep your dog's teeth sparkling white and you will both be smiling.

Paws

Your Poochon's paws are used for running, playing, playing fetch, walking or even giving you, his paw. Keep your dog's paws in tip-top shape by regularly checking them for pebbles, splinters or any other debris. Remove any splinters using a pair of tweezers and, keep the hair trimmed between his toes, otherwise it may become matted.

Paw pads can crack and bleed if they get too dry. Never use lotions or moisturizers designed for humans on your Poochon, as they will soften the pads, leading to further injury. Instead, use a high-quality, dog-formulated paw moisturizer on his feet. Give your pooch a paw massage by rubbing the moisturizer between the pads on his feet.

Winter paws – Winter is harsh on your Poochon's paws, as you have to worry about frostbite or hidden debris in the snow. Also, the salt used to melt the ice can burn your pup's paw pads, causing them to become cracked or chapped. Rock salt or other ice-melting chemicals are made from toxic chemicals that could be ingested by your pooch if he licks his paws. After coming in the house from a walk, wash your dog's paws in warm water to remove excess chemicals. Using doggy booties and limiting outdoor exposure are the best options.

Summer paws – Asphalt and pavement can get hot enough to scorch your pup's paw pads. Check the ground temperature with the palm of your hand, if you cannot rest it there comfortably for thirty seconds, then the ground is definitely too hot for your dog. Paw pads can easily become burned and blistered. If the ground is too hot, stick to grass or shady places when walking your pooch.

Ears

When grooming, it can be easy to overlook your dog's ears, but ear care is essential for Poochons. They tend to have long hairs that grow from within the ear canal, which can prevent healthy airflow or cause wax buildup. Also, your Poochon's love of water makes him more prone to bothersome ear infections.

Therefore, your Poochon's grooming routine needs to include regular ear cleaning and ear hair plucking. Plucking the ear hair is a painful solution but it is the best method as it removes both the strand and the root. However, since you have not removed the hair follicle, the hair strand will grow back. Trimming the hair strands is not recommended as the shortened, dense hairs create a trap for bacteria, yeast and debris.

How to pluck hairs from your Poochon's ears:

1. Choose a moment when both you and your Poochon are relaxed, such as when your dog has burned off some of his excess energy with a vigorous walk or a game of fetch.
2. Position your dog so you have a clear view inside of his ear. Gently bend back the ear leather, sprinkle a light dusting of dog ear powder in the ear and using the disinfected hemostat tool, grip a few hairs, lock and quickly pull up.
3. Only pluck hairs you can see, as digging around in your dog's ear can cause more damage than good. Therefore, only pull out what you can see and easily grab.
4. Throughout the entire process, use a soft, calming voice and be sure to reward your Poochon afterwards with a nice, yummy treat.

Dog ear powder – This powder is designed for plucking hairs out of your dog's ears. The powder lets you grip the strands and makes for easier removal. As this is a common problem for Poodles, there are many Poodle ear powder brands.

Hemostat – A hemostat is an essential tool designed to grip your Poochon's ear hairs; it is similar to a pair of tweezers but sturdier. It is not recommended to extract the hair strand using your fingers, as it will not extract the hair root, plus pulling the hair out with your fingers will be more painful for your dog.

Your Poochon's floppy ears can easily harbor bacteria, yeast and parasites as they create a warm, moist environment. In addition, tiny particles of debris can cause infections. Even if you regularly pluck your pup's ears there still is a risk of wax build-up. All of this needs to be regularly cleaned.

Never insert a Q-Tip in your Poochon's ears, as it could easily slip and plunge deeper in the canal, causing injury. Another word of caution: Do not clean your pup's ears too often as they could become irritated or infected.

How to clean your Poochon's ears:

1. If your Poochon's ears appear to be dirty or waxy, use a small piece of gauze or a cotton ball dampened in mineral oil or a liquid ear cleaner formulated for dogs.
2. Gently fold back your pup's ear and carefully wipe away any ear wax or debris you can see.
3. Instead of rubbing the ear to remove the debris or ear wax, gently wipe it away.

Most Poochons need to have this type of ear cleaning every two to three weeks, to keep bacteria and ear infections at bay.

Regularly check your Poochon's ears if you notice any of the following symptoms:

- Brownish or yellowish discharge
- Red and swollen inner ear canal
- Hearing loss
- Excessively shaking his head or tilting to the side
- Scabby skin around the ear flap
- Strong odor protruding from the ear
- Loss of balance
- Ear scratching or wiping his ears on the floor or rubbing his ears against the furniture

If you notice a brownish or black build-up of earwax (that looks like coffee grounds) in your Poochon's ear, he could have microscopic ear mites. Be sure to make an appointment with your vet as soon as possible.

Eyes

Check your Poochon's eyes monthly for potential symptoms, such as excessive tearing, inflammation, or cloudiness.

Photo Courtesy of Jayne Dixon

Ask your Poochon to sit in a brightly lit part of the house, preferably with natural light, and look into his eyes. Your dog's eyes should appear bright and clear, and the area surrounding the pupil should be white and not yellow. There should be no crusty, discharge on the corner of his eyes. Using your thumb, gently pull down the lower part of your dog's eyelid to observe the inner lining, it should be a pale pink color and not red or white.

On a daily basis use a clean damp cotton ball or use dog-formulated eye-wipes to wipe any gunk away from his eyes. If recommended by your vet, you can use canine eye drops to get rid of tear stains on your Poochon's eyes. Be careful not to touch your dog's eyeball.

The following symptoms are clear indications your Poochon may have an eye infection:

- Crusty gunk and discharge around the corners of his eyes
- Cloudiness
- Swollen eyelid
- Unequal pupil size
- No desire to open his eyes
- Teary eyes and tear stains

Keep the hair around your Poochon's eyes trimmed. Use a small pair of scissors, like cuticle scissors, to minimize the risk of injuring your dog. Long hair around the eyes can accidentally poke or scratch his pupils. Air conditioners will dry out your dog's eyes, causing irritation and possibly infection.

Poochon tear stains

A common issue with Poochons is the hair under or around their eyes will have a reddish, rusty brownish tint, that over time may extend down the face over the cheeks. The hairs may feel crusty, brittle, and hard to comb.

Common reasons for your Poochon's tear stains:

- Allergies
- Teething
- Unfiltered tap water
- Reactions to chemicals or additives found in poor-quality foods
- Tear duct blockage
- Ear and eye infection
- Eye lash or eye lid abnormality

Talk to your vet

The first step is to rule out any health issues such as an eye lash or eye lid abnormality, blocked tear ducts or infection. Consult with your veterinarian to rule out any potential health reasons for your Poochon's weepy eyes. The following step would be to ask your veterinarian to test your Poochon for any allergy triggers such as grass, pollen, or even wheat. If the allergies are seasonal, allergy medication can help.

Diet

If not, you may need to change your dog's diet to a grain-free, natural dog food without chemical additives. High grain content and chemical additives are one of the main reasons for tear stains, nose discoloration, and gastrointestinal issues.

Air quality

If your Poochon's allergy is external, use HEPA air filters for your central air or place air-purifiers throughout the house. Be sure to vacuum your house daily (even hardwood floors) using a vacuum with a HEPA filter to remove any allergen particles during the air exchange. Make sure everyone removes their shoes before coming into the house. Wash your Poochon's paws every time he is brought back into the house.

Say no to plastic

Studies have proven that certain brightly colored plastic food dishes can leak the artificial dye into your dog's water or food, which causes eye irritation and other maladies. If this is the cause of your Poochon's teary eyes, switch his plastic food dishes with stainless steel or ceramic dishes.

Water

Only give your Poochon filtered water. Tap water across the country contains a whole slew of harmful chemicals and carcinogens, such as mercury, fluoride, chlorine, chromium 6, lead and arsenic. If you want to ensure your pup's drinking water is safe, use a water filtering device or only offer bottled spring water.

Anal Glands

Both female and male Poochons have a pair of anal glands. They are found under the skin that surrounds your dog's anal muscles. Often, they are referred to as scent glands, odor glands, or stinky glands.

These glands hold an oily substance that is released in minute amounts when one dog meets another, which explains why they sniff each other's rear ends. The anal scent tells the other dog the dog's gender, health, and general mood. Also, the oily substance is released every time your dog has a bowel movement.

Often, when a dog is scooting his rear end on the ground after having a bowel movement, the anal sacs are engorged (swollen). Your Poochon will need your help to express his anal glands, otherwise they could become infected or even break open, which will need to be treated by your veterinarian.

How to tell if your Poochon needs his anal glands expressed:

- Scooting his rear end on the ground
- Excessively licking or biting his butt
- Red, swollen skin around his anus
- Bleeding or discharge from around the anus

Anal glands are expressed in a similar fashion as you would pop a pimple, but due to the location and the discomfort your dog is experiencing, it can be a challenge. Many pet owners prefer to ask their groomer or vet to express their dog's anal glands. If your dog's anal glands have not been expressed in quite some time, and the oily substance has become solid (impacted), then your veterinarian will need to sedate your dog for the extraction as it is very painful.

How to express your Poochon's anal glands at home:

To begin, you will need a pair of disposable latex gloves, Vaseline or a similar lubricant, paper towels, a warm soapy washcloth and someone to help you restrain your Poochon.

1. Place your dog on the table with his rear end facing you. Your dog should be standing on all fours. Have your helper gently restrain the dog, by placing one arm underneath and around your dog's neck and the other arm hugging his body.
2. Put on your latex gloves and lubricate your index finger.
3. Lift your Poochon's tail and insert your index finger about one inch into his rectum.
4. Place your thumb on the outside of your dog's anus. Using your thumb and index finger, feel for a firm pea-sized object. His anal glands should be located at the four o'clock position and at the seven o'clock position.
5. Once you have located the anal glands, using your other hand, place a paper towel in front of your dog's anus, as the glands tend to squirt outwards. Using a light pressure, gently milk the anal glands. When you can barely feel the gland, it is completely expressed. The smell is not for the faint of heart.
6. Follow the same procedure with the other gland.
7. Once you are finished draining both anal sacs, use the warm soapy wash-cloth to clean the area.
8. Reward your dog with some treats and lots of praise.

Professional Grooming

Grooming your Poochon at home gives you an excellent opportunity to bond with your pooch. But if you have ever tried to groom your dog, you know it is a whole lot trickier than it appears. However, professional groomers have the skills and knowledge to make sure your furry friend gets a stress-free haircut and grooming. After all, your Poochon deserves to be pampered!

There are pros and cons associated with at home grooming, such as less stress for your dog as he does not need to leave the comfort of his own home. It will save you money in the long run and gives you a chance to bond with your Poochon.

But on the other hand, your lack of experience can make the entire process more tedious and longer, not to mention stressful for both you and your dog. Plus, it is an investment to purchase all of the equipment needed to properly groom your dog. And let us not forget the clean up after grooming.

There are pros and cons associated with taking your dog to a professional groomer. Here is the nitty gritty:

Advantages

- Professional groomers have years of experience and can groom your dog in less time than you.
- They use professional equipment and tools, ensuring a top-notch job.
- Groomers provide specialized treatments such as de-shedding and ringworm.
- They provide a quick medical exam, and upon request they will pluck and clean your Poochon's ears and express his anal glands.
- Most groomers include nail trimming.

Disadvantages

- The cost can add up, especially if your Poochon gets groomed every six to eight weeks.
- Some Poochons suffer from anxiety and stress from being left alone at the groomers for two to three hours.
- Finding the perfect groomer for your Poochon takes time.
- Transporting your dog to and from the groomer may be troublesome if he does not enjoy long car rides.

In the end, the decision to use a professional groomer or not depends on your personal preferences and situation. Ask yourself if you have the time and patience to groom your Poochon yourself or if you can financially afford to send him regularly to the groomer.

Many dog owners prefer combining both methods in order to save money and, in the meantime, they can gain experience grooming their dog themselves at home. For example, they may get their dog professionally groomed once every four to five months and in between they will do minor grooming touch-ups and baths.

Finding a reputable groomer takes time and research.

Start your search by asking friends and family for any recommendations in your area. Once you have narrowed down your search to a few options, you will want to ask them the following questions. These questions are only a guideline. Feel free to ask any other questions that concern the well-being of your Poochon.

Can I see your facility?

The grooming facility should be clean, well-ventilated, and modern. The wash tubs and tables should be sturdy. Ask yourself as you observe the facility if you feel comfortable leaving your furry companion there. If the groomer is standoffish and refuses to let you into the facility, move on to the next option on your list.

Do they have liability?

Any reputable groomer will have liability insurance, as they will be a registered business. Using a groomer with liability coverage will give you peace of mind if your Poochon has an unfortunate accident while in the groomer's care, as any medical expenses incurred will be covered.

What is the total cost?

Never assume that one groomer will charge the same as another. Always ask what services are included in a basic grooming. Groomers often charge different fees depending on the dog's size, coat, and temperament. Often groomers offer discounts for regular dog clients.

What type of training have they received?

Many groomers are self-trained. Be sure to look for a groomer who has been professionally trained through an apprenticeship, etc. Ask the groomer how long they have been professionally grooming dogs and if they have experience grooming Poochons.

Different Hair Styles for Poochons

The Poochon is undoubtedly one of the most versatile dogs for trying out different cuts and hairstyles thanks to the volume of his coat. Below are just a few different haircuts your pooch can show off.

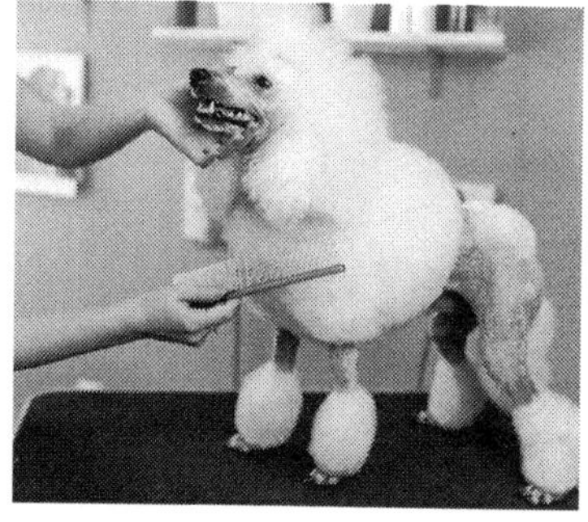

Lion's cut

The lion's cut is also called the continental haircut and is probably one of the most popular styles for Poochons. The dog's limbs are shaved, leaving only a pompom on the ankles of the front and hind legs. The tail ends with a big round pompom and the chest, stomach and head are left unshaved. This impressive cut takes a lot of time and experience to get it exactly right.

Dutch cut

The Dutch cut is one of the most popular cuts for Poochons for dog shows and competitions. Unlike the lion's cut, this cut provides a uniform style with no pompoms except for the tail as the entire coat has a uniform length. It is a very aesthetic cut, following the natural flow of the dog's body.

Puppy cut

The puppy cut is extremely popular among Poochon owners and it is not difficult to see why. This fashionable haircut makes your Poochon look like a puppy no matter his age. The front legs, chest, neck and ears have a uniform length, as the back and rear legs are shaved, except for the tail, which is left with a fluffy pompom.

Summer cut

Many Poochon owners, debate whether it is appropriate to shave off their dog's hair during the hot summer months. Summer means your Poochon will be spending more time outside, getting dirtier than usual; for this reason, a summer cut is a good idea. The summer cut basically shaves your dog's entire body except for his pompom ears and tail.

CHAPTER 13

Preventative Medical Care

By making your Poochon's health a priority, you will avoid many medical problems and increase the well-being of your furry friend. Get the facts about preventive care, vaccines, parasites, and alternative medical treatments to enhance your dog's quality of life.

Choosing a Veterinarian

Choosing a reputable veterinarian for your Poochon should not be taken lightly.

Photo Courtesy of Tanya Zahedi

Before you start checking out different veterinary clinics in your locality, make a list of your priorities for your Poochon. This will help you narrow down your options when choosing a vet and help you ask the right questions. Consider your dog's age, family history (if known), and any health concerns. For example, if your furry friend is getting older, look for a vet who specializes in geriatric care.

Here is a basic checklist of essential requirements for veterinarians (requirements may vary depending on your dog's needs):

- Proximity to your house -If there is an emergency can you get to the veterinary clinic quickly?
- Pricing – Every veterinary clinic has different prices; make sure the clinic you choose fits your budget.
- Do the clinic's hours work with your work schedule or will you need to take time off to take your Poochon there?
- Does it have up-to-date facilities with cutting edge medical technologies and care?
- Check for generous appointment times, as you do not want to feel rushed during the visit.
- A smaller practice means you most likely see the same vet every time you visit, plus your Poochon can develop a rapport with the medical staff.
- Does the staff have knowledge of alternative and holistic treatments?
- Is the staff involved in the local animal welfare community, such as pet rescue organizations?

Once you have narrowed down what you want from a veterinarian, it is time to search for a few candidates. The best place to start is by word of mouth. Ask fellow dog owners, whose pet care philosophies are in line with your own, about their vets. Or ask a friend or family member for recommendations. Many veterinarian clinics offer a referral program which mean discounts for you and your friend who referred you.

If you are new to an area, you can check the American Animal Hospital Association (AAHA) website, you will find a list of accredited veterinarians in your locality as well as an evaluation of the facility, staff, patient care, and equipment.

Whether you get a referral from a friend or from an online search, you will want to make sure the veterinarian clinic is accredited with the AAHA. The AAHA regularly evaluates veterinary practices throughout the United States on their standard for patient care, pain management, facilities, surgery, medical records, cleanliness, anesthesiology, and more. Unfortunately, veterinary clinics are not required to be accredited by law, but accreditation shows you their philosophies are committed to maintaining only the highest standard of care or service.

When you finally narrow the list down to one or two veterinary practices, you should ask to take a tour of the facility. Any reputable vet will be more than happy to show you around and make you feel comfortable. One of the main aspects to observe is if the staff is caring, calm and courteous. Another important aspect is the cleanliness of the lobby, waiting rooms, and exam rooms.

In addition to getting a feel for the facility, ask plenty of questions. Vets appreciate when pet owners are interested in their pet's health and well-being.

Here are some questions you should ask when interviewing the vet:

- How are overnight patients monitored?
- Are all diagnostic tests like bloodwork, ultrasounds, X-rays, etc. done on-site or in another referred location?
- Are all of the veterinary technicians employed by the clinic licensed by the state to practice on animals?
- Does the facility refer patients to specialists if needed? (Their answer should be affirmative.)
- What types of payment plans does the practice accept? Are there special payment plans for major surgeries or treatments?

The questions above are simply a guideline. Feel free to ask any other questions that concern you and your Poochon.

The in-person visit should leave you with a positive feeling about the practice and the staff. Communication is a vital part of quality health care for your Poochon, as he cannot explain to the doctor where it hurts; it is up to you to do the talking. So, you need to feel comfortable asking questions to the vet.

Once you have chosen a vet, be a good client. Show up early for appointments to allot time to fill out any necessary paperwork, etc. Be your Poochon's advocate, but know when to step back and let the vet take over. Be patient; emergencies may take precedence over routine appointments.

If you have problems with your vet, do not hesitate to switch facilities. Veterinary clinics expect clients to come and go. However, before you depart, be sure to request a complete copy of your Poochon's medical file. You can ask that your dog's health records be faxed or mailed to either you or the new vet.

Photo Courtesy of Claire Hill

Microchipping

Each year, more than eight million pets end up in a shelter across the country and fewer than twenty percent are reclaimed.

A microchip is about the size of a grain of rice. It is implanted in your Poochon's neck and your dog will not even notice it is there. An average cost to get your dog microchipped costs around $30 to $50, depending on your vet.

Generally, the entire process takes only a few seconds or about the time it takes to give your dog an injection. It will take more time for you to fill out all of the paperwork involved than it will to insert the microchip! Microchipping does not necessarily have to be completed by a vet, but it is highly recommended you use a vet's service.

If your dog is squeamish around injections and needles, you might want to consider getting him chipped at the same time he is being neutered. Most pet owners opt to have their pooches chipped when they are spayed or neutered for this very reason. The pain is similar to using a needle to draw blood; some dogs flinch, others do not.

If your Poochon happens to get lost, he may have on his collar and ID tags, but if your dog is a victim of theft, the thief will most likely remove the collar and ID tags and toss them in the trash. Whereas, with a microchip the people who find your dog can take him in to be scanned either at a local shelter or vet's office, so you can be reunited with your Poochon. Or if someone else says your dog is their dog because they purchased it from the thief, you can prove the dog is yours.

Pet doors can be programmed to recognize your dog's microchip, letting him come into the house but keeping other animals outside. However, a microchip will not prevent your Poochon from being accidentally hit by a car, so never let him run loose.

One of the biggest misconceptions about microchips is that your dog can be tracked. In order to know your Poochon's whereabouts, the chip will need to be scanned. Trust me, you will never regret getting your dog chipped, but if your pooch gets lost, you will always regret that you did not.

Neutering and Spaying

There are numerous caring and health-conscious reasons to spay or neuter your furry canine friend.

Spaying is a simple surgical procedure performed by your veterinarian which involves removing your female dog's ovaries and uterus. Here are some reasons why you should consider spaying your Poochon:

- Spaying reduces the risk of urinary infections and breast cancer. It is highly recommended to spay your Poochon before her first heat to prevent health complications in the future.

Photo Courtesy of Jenny Choudhury

- If your unspayed Poochon accidentally mates with a larger dog, her uterus may be too small to accommodate the litter and could rupture, causing serious injury. Spaying limits this risk.
- Spaying prevents unwanted pregnancies, which saves you from unplanned expenses.
- A spayed dog will not go into heat. A female dog in heat will urinate all over the house and yowl loudly while trying to attract a mate.

Neutering is a simple surgical procedure performed by your veterinarian which involves removing your male dog's testicles. Here are some reasons why you should consider neutering your Poochon:

- Neutering prevents testicular cancer.
- Your Poochon will not roam about the neighborhood in search of a mate. An unneutered male dog will do everything in his power to find a mate, including digging a hole under the fence or running across a busy highway.
- A neutered dog will be less aggressive and better behaved than an unneutered dog. Also, he will not have the desire to mark his territory by spraying urine everywhere.

Neutered and spayed Poochons are both much better behaved as they will focus their undivided attention on their human family instead of finding a mate. Many aggression issues are eliminated when your pet is neutered or spayed.

Many concerns you may have about getting your dog spayed or neutered are just misinformation. Consider the following:

Will your dog feel remorse or loss? No. Dogs do not suffer from emotional insecurities or experience societal pressures to have a family like humans do. They do not need to procreate to feel emotionally fulfilled.

Does spaying or neutering cause obesity? Contrary to popular belief, spaying and neutering will not make your Poochon fat. However, a lack of exercise and over-feeding will.

Are there negative side effects? As with all surgical procedures, there are certain risks, but these are minor and rare, and often occur when the procedure is not performed by a reputable veterinarian.

Many states and countries have established low-cost programs for spaying or neutering, which makes these types of surgeries an affordable option for all pet owners. The webpage for the Humane Society will provide you with a list of local, affordable clinic and funding options to help you cover the cost of the procedure. If you are not planning on professionally breeding your Poochon, then you should definitely consider getting your Poochon neutered or spayed.

Vaccinations

Vaccinating your Poochon is a necessity if you want to give him a long and healthy life. Your veterinarian will help you determine a vaccine regime for your Poochon by taking into consideration his health, lifestyle and area where you live.

Vaccinations are designed to help your dog fight off organisms that cause diseases. Vaccines are made up of antigens, which the immune system identifies as the same disease-ridden organism, but without actually causing your dog to become sick. When the vaccine is introduced into the body, it is instructing the immune system how to fight off the real virus in its entirety, hence building antibodies.

The American Animal Hospital Association (AAHA) recommends all dogs receive core vaccines throughout their lives. Your veterinarian may recommend other noncore vaccines depending on the geography, lifestyle and the current prevalence of the disease. For example, a noncore vaccine for kennel cough is required for dogs who frequent doggie daycare, a kennel, grooming facilities, and so on.

Puppies – A puppy's mother will pass on antibodies while nursing her pups. When puppies are six to eight weeks of age, they will receive a series of three core vaccines administered by a veterinarian with three-to-four-week intervals. The final dose should be administered when your Poochon is sixteen weeks of age.

Adult dogs – Depending on your Poochon's lifestyle, he will require annual vaccines or booster shots every two to three years.

Rabies – It is mandatory throughout the United States for all dogs to be vaccinated against rabies. However, each state and county have different laws regarding the administration of rabies vaccines. For example, some states require an annual vaccine while others need doses once every three years.

The majority of dogs experience no side effects from being vaccinated. However, there are exceedingly rare cases of severe side effects caused from a vaccine. But as with any type of medical procedure, there can be complications and risks involved. Reactions are often short-lived and rarely require veterinary care. Here is a list of common reactions:

- Lack of appetite
- Sluggishness
- Vomiting
- Swelling, pain, redness or hair loss around the injection site
- Fever
- Diarrhea

Schedule your Poochon's vaccinations when you will be around to monitor him for a few days. If your dog experiences any severe symptoms, like seizures, difficulty breathing or lameness, call your vet as soon as possible.

Internal Parasites

Internal parasites may be parasites or worms. The idea of your dog having creepy crawlies moving about inside of their internal organs is always unpleasant. But understanding the symptoms, risks, and treatment options is part of being a responsible puppy parent.

If internal parasites or worms in dogs are left untreated, they can cause serious, long-term health problems for your pooch. These types of parasites can be passed to your dog from contaminated soil or other dog's stool, and certain types of worms may even infect humans.

There are five main types of worms that commonly affect Poochons: hookworms, whipworms, heartworms, roundworms and tapeworms. By familiarizing yourself with these common parasites you will learn how to keep your dog safe. While each parasite affects dogs differently, there are some general warning signs that your Poochon may have parasites:

- Abdominal pain
- Vomiting
- Diarrhea that lasts longer than twenty-four hours
- Unexplained weight loss
- Pot-bellied appearance
- Extreme lethargy
- Dehydration
- Poor coat appearance, hair loss or hot spots
- Coughing

Here are some common internal parasites that may affect your dog:

Roundworms – Roundworms are one of the most common types of internal parasite in dogs, and can be transmitted to humans. Many puppies are born with roundworms as it was passed on from their mother. Roundworms can be diagnosed by your vet with a small fecal sample and treated with deworming medications. If left untreated, roundworms can cause your puppy to become anemic, retard growth, and may be fatal in some cases.

Whipworms – Whipworms live in the large intestine and colon. Dogs can become infected by whipworms by consuming an infested substance, such as fecal matter, soil, food, water, or animal flesh. Eggs can survive in soil up to five years, which is another reason to clean up after your pooch when he relieves himself. Severe cases of whipworms can cause weight loss, inflammation, diarrhea, and anemia. Often three-monthly treatments will be required to eliminate whipworms.

Tapeworms – Tapeworms are intestinal parasites that are often transmitted through a flea bite or by consuming dead animals or fleas infested with tapeworms. When a dog consumes a flea infested with tapeworm eggs, the egg will attach itself to the dog's intestines and hatch. Infected dogs may scoot their rear end on the ground.

Often, in infected dogs stool pieces of the tapeworm may break off and resemble small pieces of rice. If you suspect your Poochon has tapeworms, take a stool sample to your vet for diagnosis. Treatment involves an oral medicine, an injection, and fumigating your house for fleas. Infected flea bites may infect humans.

Hookworms – Hookworms can be fatal in puppies if left untreated. There are several types of hookworms that attach themselves to the dog's intestinal wall to gorge themselves on blood, causing anemia. Your dog can get hookworms from ingesting contaminated fecal matter or they can be passed on to puppies through their mother's milk. Humans can become infected with hookworms. Treatment involves a deworming medication which will need to be administered twice.

Heartworms – Heartworms are transmitted through a mosquito bite, but can be easily prevented by giving your dog regular heartworm medication. Heartworms grow and multiply at an extraordinary rate inside of your dog's heart, causing heart disease, heart failure, organ damage, and ultimately a painful death. Mosquitos carrying the heartworm parasite can be found in all fifty states.

The best approach to heartworms is prevention, as treating heartworms is extremely expensive and can have serious side effects. Also, treating heartworms requires keeping your dog confined without exercise for long periods of time in order to prevent heart damage. Even if your dog is regularly taking heartworm preventives, he will need to be tested regularly for worms.

How to diagnose worms

Some internal parasites, such as tapeworms may be observed in your dog's fecal matter. However, most parasites will need to be diagnosed by your vet via a microscopic examination of the stool sample. If your dog exhibits any of the symptoms listed above, your vet will ask you to bring in a stool sample. Even if there are no symptoms, it is wise to take a stool sample with you to your dog's annual check-up.

Your vet will set up a regular deworming schedule for your Poochon to treat different types of intestinal parasites, as well as preventive heartworm medication. The bottom line – prevention, flea control, and regular testing are the best actions to prevent consequences caused by internal parasites.

Fleas and Ticks

Your Poochon's soft, warm coat provides the ideal environment to harbor ticks and fleas. These insects feed on your dog's blood and may cause health problems ranging from allergic reactions to serious life-threatening illnesses caused from a tick bite. Despite the fact that fleas and ticks are more common during the warmer months, you will need to ward them off year-round.

Fleas – One of the most common external parasites, not only affects your dog but, they can also set up home inside of your house. These blood-sucking insects have the ability to jump almost three feet and can survive in even the harshest environments. An average lifespan for a flea may be anywhere from twelve days to an entire year. During that time, they can produce millions of baby fleas, which will produce even more offspring.

Symptoms your Poochon has fleas:

- Hair loss
- Allergic dermatitis
- Flea droppings can be found throughout your Poochon's coat. Use a fine-tooth comb, especially around his abdomen, ears, mouth and tail. Flea droppings look like tiny dirt particles or sand
- Flea eggs, look like white grains of sand
- Excessive biting, licking or scratching
- Hot spots or scabs

Fleas are expert stowaways. They quickly attach themselves to animals while outside or can jump from one dog to another. If not controlled, fleas can invade your house within a day or two.

If not controlled, fleas can cause serious health complications for their host. For example, a flea consumes approximately fifteen times their body weight in blood each day, causing your Poochon to become anemic. Some dogs have an allergic reaction to flea bites, which is called allergic dermatitis.

If your Poochon has fleas, all your resident pets will need to be treated. Also, your indoor environment will need to be fumigated to keep off any pesky fleas and their eggs. Your veterinarian will be able to confirm your suspicions, and most likely will suggest one or two of the following treatments:

- Oral or topical treatment or dog-formulated shampoo for your Poochon.
- Thoroughly cleaning your house, including bedding, rugs and upholstery. A severe infestation will require professional help, which means you and all your pets will have to temporarily evacuate your home.
- If your Poochon gets re-infested every time he goes into the backyard, you may need to fumigate your lawn.

Photo Courtesy of Alexandra Costello

Flea prevention:

- Wash your Poochon's bedding at least once a week in hot, soapy water and brush him using a flea brush.
- Rake up any grass clippings or leaves in your backyard, as fleas tend to conceal themselves in dark, moist areas.
- There are preventive flea-control measures available either by prescription or over-the-counter. Be aware some flea collars can be carcinogenic for animals and humans. Always consult with your vet beforehand.

Ticks -Ticks are considered to be a parasite as they feed on the host's blood. Ticks are experts at concealing themselves by burrowing into their hosts then gorging on their blood. Ticks can transmit a long list of serious diseases. Transmission varies by certain areas and climates. Ask your vet what types of ticks are in your locality.

Ticks are most active during late spring and early summer. Ticks prefer to burrow themselves into their host's head, neck, ears and feet but can be found in other places. Ticks jump from one animal to another.

How to check your Poochon for ticks:

Ticks are about the size of a pinhead and are not often noticed until they bite your dog and begin to swell up with blood. If you live in an area where ticks are prevalent, be sure to regularly check your dog. Carefully run your fingers through his coat, paying extra attention to warm spots, such as inside of his ears, in his feet and on his head. Repeat this every time he comes inside from playing outside.

Health complications caused by ticks:

- Blood loss and anemia
- Tick paralysis
- Allergic dermatitis
- Lyme disease – Deer ticks are the primary carrier of Lyme disease, which causes depression, fever, loss of appetite, painful joints, and kidney failure and needs to be treated with antibiotics.

If you find a tick attached to your Poochon, it is important to be careful when removing it as the tick's blood could infect your dog or you, if you accidentally come into contact with it.

Follow these instructions to safely remove the tick:

1. Prepare a glass jar with rubbing alcohol inside; this is where you will place the tick. This allows you to take the tick in for testing at your vet-

erinary clinic. Put on latex gloves and ask a family member to distract your Poochon while you extract the tick.

2. Using a pair of disinfected tweezers, gently grasp the tick as close as you can to the dog's skin. Pull straight upwards using even pressure then place the tick into the jar with rubbing alcohol. Do not twist the tick out, as this could leave the head attached inside the dog or cause the tick to regurgitate infected fluids.
3. Disinfect the bitten area and the tweezers; wash your hands with warm, soapy water afterwards. Monitor the area for the next few weeks for any signs of an infection. If there is a sign of infection, take your Poochon and the tick to the veterinarian for a check-up.

Many products used to treat or to prevent fleas are also useful in killing ticks.

Keep your yard tick-free by keeping the grass cut and by removing any large weeds that could be hiding places for ticks.

Holistic Alternatives and Supplements

Holistic veterinary care is a new term that can easily be misunderstood. Often holistic care is combined with conventional medicine to treat injury or disease to aid the dog's healing process. For example, if your Poochon had surgery for a hip replacement, he will need to take medications to fight off infection. But some veterinarians recommend using a holistic treatment such as acupuncture or massages, to naturally ease the pain and hasten the healing process.

Below you can find a list of some of the most popular holistic treatments used by concerned pet parents. Some of these treatments have been scientifically proven. If you have doubts or questions as to what type of treatment is best suited for your Poochon, be sure to discuss the options over with your veterinarian to find the best alternative and conventional treatment for your dog.

Canine acupuncture

Acupuncture uses needles to stimulate pressure points to release the buildup of certain chemicals in the muscles, spinal cord and brain, thus promoting better health. There is plenty of anecdotal proof that acupuncture can relieve dogs of joint and muscle pain, encourage healing post-surgery and even treat cancer or other types of trauma.

Hydrotherapy

Hydrotherapy in layman terms means physical therapy in water. This type of therapy is highly recommended for dogs in need of a low-impact exercise due to joint pain due to arthritis or recovery from an injury or surgery. Hydrotherapy is proven to build muscle, improve mobility, decrease stress, and increase circulation.

Chinese herbal medicine

Chinese herbal medicine has mastered the art of combining certain herbs to relieve pain, improve and restore organ function, and strengthen the immune system. Many pet owners rave about Chinese herbal medicine as they have seen their pup's physical and emotional improvement with the use of the herbs. As with all herbs, make sure they are safe to use alongside your dog's conventional medications, such as blood thinners or diuretics.

Magnetic field therapy

According to the Veterinary Clinics of America, magnet therapy is gaining popularity in the United States to treat illness and injury, however, there is not much evidence that the application of magnets can heal your Poochon. Magnet field therapy is affordable, non-invasive and virtually has no side effects.

Canine massage

Canine massage encourages healing, improves circulation, stimulates nerves, relieves stress and relaxes your dog's muscles. One of the biggest advantages to a doggy massage is that it makes your pooch feel good and strengthens the bond between a person and the dog. Massages will not cure your Poochon's cancer or injury; it will, however, make him feel relaxed and loved.

Nutritional supplements

Nutritional supplements are required if you are feeding your dog a homemade or raw diet to make up for any nutritional deficiencies. Look for nutritional supplements that include calcium, Omega fatty acids, vitamins, and amino acids.

When choosing a holistic treatment or supplement for your dog, be sure to use good judgment and always consult prior with your veterinarian to see if the treatment will help your dog. Note Just because an herbal substance states it is healthy and beneficial, it does not mean that it is harmless. Always thoroughly research a product before giving it to your dog.

Dog Depression

Dogs, like humans, experience depression. However, they cannot simply tell us that they are feeling sad or depressed. Currently there is not as much research out there about dog depression as there is for humans, but there is plenty of unofficial data pointing to the fact that dog depression does exist.

Often doggy depression is obvious, such as when your Poochon sleeps all day in the dark corner of the laundry room when another furry friend dies from the household. Other symptoms may not be so straightforward, as your dog may be moping around the house after a move to a new area.

How can you tell if your Poochon has canine depression? You will be surprised to discover many of the symptoms are quite similar to humans.

HELPFUL TIP
Cushing's Syndrome

While a Poochon's health will largely be determined by the health and genetics of the dog's parents, there are several diseases that Poochons may be predisposed to. One of these is called Cushing's Syndrome, and it happens when your dog produces too much of the hormone cortisol. Cortisol plays an important role in many bodily functions, but too much of this hormone can cause issues. Identifying this syndrome can be tricky because the symptoms can mimic other diseases, and diagnosis requires testing by your veterinarian. Symptoms can include increased thirst or hunger, bathroom accidents, excess hair loss, panting, fatigue, potbelly, and skin infections. If you notice any concerning changes in your dog, don't hesitate to discuss these changes with your vet. Cushing's Syndrome can often be treated with medication.

Changes in appetite – Some pups lose interest in food when they become extremely sad, and start losing weight. Alternatively, other dogs may use food as a type of solace when they are feeling blue, which leads to weight gain.

Sleeping all day long – Poochons love to sleep, especially when they are snuggled up beside you on the couch. However, if you notice your pooch continues to sleep long after you got home, barely reacting to your presence, then it is a warning sign something is wrong. If you cannot find any physical problems, then your dog may be depressed.

Lack of interest -If your Poochon begins to lose interest in activities that he used to love, such as playing fetch or going for walks, then take note. Dogs who begin to slow down or lose interest in everyday activities may be experiencing canine depression.

Excessive licking – Excessive paw licking may be a sign of deep-rooted psychological issues. Research has proven that dogs will lick or chew their paws to comfort themselves.

Avoidance and hiding – When a dog hides, it can be one of two things – illness or injury (with depression being included under the illness category). If your dog is avoiding his human family and hiding himself it could mean that something is upsetting him. If there is no physical reason, then it is emotional.

Never assume your Poochon is depressed. First, get your veterinarian to rule out that any physical or medical reasons are causing his change in behavior. Then, if medical issues are ruled out, your vet will give you suggestions to help your furry friend beat the blues.

Pet Insurance

No matter how cautious you are with your Poochon, unwanted accidents happen – and often they are expensive.

Veterinary costs are higher than ever. According to the American Pet Product Association, an average dog owner spends an average of $248 for annual check-ups. What happens when the unexpected occurs? Costs can add up even more! For example, a typical corrective surgical procedure, such as cataracts for a senior dog, can cost $1,200 and up. Foreign-body ingestions can cost a whopping $3,600 without insurance.

Pet insurance can help to defray these costs. Currently, more than fifteen different insurance companies in the United States offer pet insurance, but less than one percent of dog owners purchases this type of insurance.

Here are a few benefits and drawbacks of pet insurance:

- Gives you peace of mind knowing you have the resources for any unforeseen medical costs if your Poochon becomes injured or ill.
- Pet insurance gives vets the opportunity to give your pooch top-notch care without having to worry about incurring too many medical costs for you.
- Pet insurance helps your dog live a longer and healthier life, as you will not hesitate to take your dog in for medical treatment before his condition worsens.

- Some insurance companies look at factors such as the dog's age, whether she is a purebred or a designer breed dog, and the dog's living environment. Depending on these factors, the monthly insurance could increase.

- Many insurance companies have a waiting period such as 48-hour period before approving accident insurance and 14-day waiting period before approval for illnesses.
- Depending on the fine print of the insurance plan, it may exclude pre-existing illnesses, pregnancy and/or birth, routine vaccines, and dental maintenance.
- The majority of pet insurance plans require you pay for the entire veterinary cost up front and afterwards, submit a claim for reimbursement.

The final price of pet insurance depends on the age of your Poochon and the type of coverage you choose. Pet insurance works similarly to human health insurance. Once you choose a plan that works for you and your Poochon, you can expect to pay a monthly premium of about $20 to $50. The deductible depends on the insurance plan you finally choose.

Note: Your pet insurance will be void if your Poochon is not up-to-date on his vaccinations and deworming. Also, if your dog gets sick from something that is preventable from being vaccinated, most insurance companies will not cover the expenses.

Unfortunately, there is no right or wrong answer regarding whether or not you should buy pet insurance for your Poochon. If you do opt to purchase the coverage, as with all insurance plans, be sure to read the fine print very carefully.

Consider Self-Insuring

If you feel pet insurance is too costly for your monthly budget, then another practical option is to set up a personal saving account for your Poochon. You can always deposit an established amount into the account on a monthly basis and only withdraw it for medical care for your dog. This is only a good option if you are disciplined with money.

The bottom line – veterinary care can add up quickly, especially if your pooch needs costly diagnostics, care, and treatment. If you decide to purchase pet insurance, be sure to read the fine print to understand exactly what you are getting yourself into.

CHAPTER 14

Caring for a Senior Poochon

Your Poochon has become more than a four-legged companion. He is part of your immediate family. Just as your pooch has cared about you over the years, you want to care for him throughout his life, even more so as he ages. Dogs age quite similarly to humans. They too, lose control of their physical and mental abilities.

As your Poochon ages, you are going to notice some changes such as slowing down, decreased agility and mobility, and personality changes. Perhaps your pooch has become less enthusiastic about his favorite activities, such as going for walks, eating or even playing a game of fetch. But, with love and care, you can help your Poochon age gracefully.

Photo Courtesy of Kj and Philip Lynn

Physical and Mental Signs of Aging

It is a well-known fact that dogs age faster than their pet owners. Generally, a smaller breed like your Poochon enters the senior years around seven or eight of our years. The more aware you are of the typical signs of aging, the sooner you can make your pup's later years more comfortable.

Here are some common physical and mental signs of aging your Poochon may experience:

- Bathroom issues
- Hearing loss
- Mobility issues
- New lumps and bumps
- Aches and pains
- Poor vision
- Stinky breath
- Weight change

As your Poochon ages, you will also notice behavioral changes. Changes in your dog's temperament and behavior may be an indication of physical issues. For example, your normally mellow friend could suddenly turn into an old grouch. He may be in pain from arthritis. Or maybe your hyperactive Poochon suddenly wants to sleep all day long. Senior dogs need more rest so - let him sleep.

Your senior Poochon may also begin to display cognitive symptoms, such as forgetting where his water dish is or simply barking at nothing. Your dog may seem to be going senile, which is entirely possible as dogs can develop cognitive problems just like humans. Many behavioral changes are caused by canine cognitive dysfunction syndrome (CCDS). CCDS is similar to Alzheimer's disease and affects around half of all dogs over 11 years of age.

At around 15 years of age, almost 70% of all dogs begin to experience symptoms associated with CCDS. Some behavioral changes your Poochon might display are:

- House soiling
- Increased anxiety
- Fear of familiar people and objects
- Compulsive behaviors
- Excessive barking and vocalization

- Change in activity level
- Insomnia, sleep-walking, or restlessness

If you observe your Poochon displaying any of these symptoms, consult with your vet. Your vet will make a diagnosis by asking you a few questions during the visit. There is no cure for CCDS, however there are medications and therapeutic options.

Illness and Injury Prevention

Strained muscles, sprains, and pulled ligaments are all common senior canine injuries. As your Poochon ages, he will become more susceptible to injury due to brittle bones and arthritis. Research shows dogs experience a similar pain threshold as that of humans. You can easily reduce injuries by incorporating these strategies into your dog's daily life.

Avoid extreme temperatures – Elderly Poochons are more sensitive to extreme temperature changes. They can suffer more easily from heatstroke, frostbite, and hypothermia than younger dogs. If the weather outside is too hot or too cold, keep your pooch inside.

Daily exercise schedule – Even though your senior Poochon has gotten slower in the last few years, that does not mean he does not need regular exercise. Switch up your dog's exercise routine by taking him for shorter walks. Instead of walking on cement, take your canine for a walk on a dirt or grass path, as it will be softer on his sore joints.

Ramp up – Climbing stairs, jumping up on the couch, or getting into the car may become a challenge for your senior dog. At your local pet supply store, you can find a variety of ramps to help your pooch with these movements.

Slip proof your home – Your Poochon may lack the agility he once had during his younger years. Your hardwood or tile floors may cause him to slip and slide causing injury. Place rugs in areas your dog tends to spend the majority of his time as it will help him feel more secure and sure-footed.

Soft, fluffy bed – Your Poochon will thank you for a soft, fluffy bed that supports his old bones and joints. Invest in a doggy bed with soft sides, so your senior pooch can rest his head on a soft surface while he observes his surroundings.

Take it slow – Your elderly Poochon will need extra time for eating, walking, going to the bathroom, etc. Be patient with him and give him the time he needs. Your furry friend also will appreciate any extra attention, love, and affection from you, like cuddling on the couch.

Weight control – Since your senior Poochon is less active, he is burning fewer calories meaning unwanted weight gain. Extra weight puts pressure on your old dog's bones, joints and heart, which could cause additional health problems. Consult with your vet for recommendations to improve your dog's diet.

Signs of illness or pain

Each dog will display pain and suffering differently. Any change in your Poochon's behavior may be an early indication that he is ill or in pain.

When your dog is in pain or is ill, his eating or drinking habits will often change. He might lose interest in food or even drink excessive amounts of water. He may become withdrawn, be aggressive when petted, or seem unwilling to go for a walk. Your dog may display one or more of these signs of ill health:

- Runny nose, eyes or discharge coming from the ears
- Excessive drooling
- Vomiting
- Diarrhea
- Constipation
- Difficulty urinating
- Coughing
- Hot spots, excessive scratching or skin sores under his coat
- Limping, swelling and lack of mobility

If you notice that your Poochon is displaying any of these symptoms for more than forty-eight hours, consult with your veterinarian about any health issues.

Age-Related Diseases and Conditions in Poochons

During your Poochon's golden years, he may begin to experience age-associated illnesses and diseases. Many of these conditions can be treated if identified early, so be sure to consult with your vet immediately. The following health issues are commonly associated with geriatric Poochons.

Arthritis – Just like people, dogs develop arthritis as they age. The most common type of arthritis in aging Poochons is osteoarthritis, also called degenerative joint disease. This condition affects the hips, knees, shoulders, and elbows. The changes in joints result in pain, stiffness, and lack of mobility. Osteoarthritis is progressive, meaning there is no cure but there are many treatments, such as chiropractic, hydrotherapy and acupuncture, which are known to slow the progression and ease the joint pain.

Cancer - Unfortunately, cancer is common in older dogs. Different types of cancer can cause a variety of symptoms. Often, symptoms may be dismissed as signs of aging, such as lethargy or a lack of appetite. As your Poochon ages, it is vital he receives routine wellness screenings with your vet. Lab work, additional diagnostic imaging, and exams can pick up on anything that is unseen to the naked eye. The sooner the cancer is caught, the better the chances of your dog's survival.

Cataracts – Cataracts cause your Poochon's eye to lose transparency, causing them to appear cloudy. The cataract prevents light from passing through your dog's lens, blocking his vision. Most elderly dogs who develop cataracts will not completely go blind and they adjust to their loss in vision. Your vet will need to diagnose the cause of the cataract before coming up with a treatment plan.

Glaucoma –Your dog's eye is made up of a jelly-like substance called aqueous humor. This liquid is constantly being produced by the eye. Normally, the eye drains itself of the old fluid, but if this does not occur then glaucoma happens. Glaucoma in dogs can have one of many causes, so be sure to consult with your vet to find the correct treatment for your dog.

Hypothyroidism – Hypothyroidism is common in older Poochons as their thyroid gland becomes weaker and underactive. One of the main indications of hypothyroidism is unexplained weight gain, lack of interest in playing or going for walks, and separation anxiety. Additional symptoms are brittle hair and itchy skin. The good news is that this condition can be easily treated with prescription medications.

Diabetes – Poochons are prone to developing canine diabetes. Diabetes occurs when the pancreas stops producing normal amounts of insulin and may be caused from an inherited predisposition, diet, obesity, and certain medications such as steroids used for treating allergies. Diabetes can easily be regulated with insulin shots and a change in diet.

Incontinence – Age takes a toll on your dog's organs, muscles, and nerves, making it more challenging to hold it the way he used to. Incontinence may be an indication of another health complications, so you will need your vet to rule out some issues first. If the vet does not find any health problems, you may need to let your Poochon out more often for potty breaks or have him wear a doggy diaper.

Kidney Disease – Kidney disease often develops slowly, starting off as renal insufficiency and progressing to full renal failure. Once this disease

Photo Courtesy of Julliete Abrahamson

starts to progress, there is no cure, but if caught in time it can be successfully treated to slow the progression. Signs of kidney disease include increased thirst, frequent urination, lack of appetite, vomiting, and lethargy.

Lenticular Sclerosis – This condition is often confused with cataracts as it also causes the dog's eyes to form a white, cloudy reflection. Lenticular sclerosis, however, does not affect your Poochon's vision. But to be on the safe side, get your dog's eyes checked out by your vet.

Muscle Atrophy – Muscle atrophy is common in older Poochons as they become less active with age. This condition causes rear leg weakness, limping, ataxia, paw dragging, flabby muscles and weight loss. Muscle atrophy can be caused from a number of conditions such as arthritis, injury, and sore muscles from lack of exercise. Your vet will need to give your dog a checkup to diagnose the cause of your Poochon's muscle atrophy before treating it.

Nutrition Needs

Every Poochon has different nutritional needs, and senior dogs are no exception. Once your pooch reaches his golden years, it can become a challenge to understand his new dietary requirements. However, switching your dog's regular dog food for a bag of senior dog food may not be enough.

Watch those calories – Younger senior dogs tend to gain weight while older senior dogs tend to lose weight. As your pooch ages, he begins to slow down which means he burns off fewer calories and those unneeded calories are stored as fat. Research shows senior dogs require 20% fewer calories than an adult dog in order to maintain a healthy weight. If your Poochon starts losing weight, you may need to give him extra calories to help him stay healthy.

Nutrient rich dog food – Even though your Poochon may require fewer calories, he will need a premium diet that provides all of the required nutrients to stay healthy. Recent studies have discovered that food rich in L-carnitine helps elderly dogs to burn off stored fat for energy. So, make sure your Poochon receives a diet rich in lean red meats, chicken, fish, healthy fats, and dairy products.

Protein – Protein is vital for your Poochon's overall health. As your dog ages, he begins to lose muscle mass, even if he is still leading an active lifestyle. As his muscle mass depletes, so does his protein reserve, causing his immune system to weaken. As your dog's immune system weakens, so does his ability to fight off infections and illnesses. Your senior Poochon's diet should be made up of 40% protein. Avoid dog foods that contain fillers. Instead, opt for foods rich in lean red meats, fish, chicken, and dairy products.

Fiber – Fiber is essential in helping your Poochon lose weight, alleviating constipation and controlling blood sugar levels. However, certain cellulose-based fibers are difficult for your dog to digest and prevent other nutrients from being absorbed. Avoid giving your dog foods that contain bran flakes, psyllium husks, and dried peas. Research shows soluble fibers help senior dogs regulate glucose levels and absorb nutrients better. Some beneficial soluble fibers for your dog are sweet potatoes, carrots, brown rice, milled flaxseed, wheatgerm, kale and kelp.

Sodium – Your senior Poochon will need a low-sodium diet if he has hypertension, cardiac, or kidney problems. Most commercial dog food is extremely high in sodium so look for brands that are low in sodium or make your own homemade dog food.

If your senior Poochon will not eat

It is common for senior dogs to lose interest in food. Try adding one to two tablespoons of bone broth or a small amount of canned food to entice your dog. If your elderly pooch refuses to eat for more than forty-eight hours, consult with your vet to rule out any underlying health problems.

Bone broth is a delicious, nutrient-dense superfood that will improve your Poochon's health and guaranteed to get him to gobble up his dinner. The bone broth is a stock made from simmering raw bones for several hours, either in your slow-cooker or on low-heat on your stove top. Bone broth is jam-packed with nutrients that will improve your dog's overall health, plus he will devour his food.

How to make bone broth for your Poochon:

Ingredients

- 4 pounds of raw bones with marrow (you can use chicken, turkey, rabbit, beef or oxtail bones)
- 1/3 cup fresh parsley, chopped
- 3 stalks of celery, chopped
- 1/4 cup organic apple cider vinegar (helps to pull the marrow and minerals out of the bones)
- 6 to 7 quarts of water

1. Place all of the ingredients in a large pot or the slow cooker.
2. Cook on low heat for 8 to 12 hours on a low simmer or for 24 hours in the slow cooker on the lowest setting. Stir occasionally and add extra water if necessary.
3. Allow to cool. Remove the bones, celery, parsley and discard. Note you should never feed cooked bones to your Poochon.

4. Once the broth is completely cool, place in the refrigerator overnight. It will form a layer of fat on top which can easily be skimmed off and discarded.
5. Freeze in small portions in zip-lock baggies, then thaw before serving your Poochon. Give him one to two tablespoons with each meal.

How to choose a premium senior dog food

Unfortunately, the FDA has not established any official regulations for senior dog foods, which is why you need to educate yourself on how to find a premium-quality dog food for your Poochon.

Beyond the caloric intake and protein content, there are several ingredients that can benefit your Poochon's overall health. Here are a few key ingredients to look for when choosing a premium dog food.

Glucosamine and Chondroitin – These supplements help your senior dog's cartilage and joints so he can move around with less pain.

Antioxidants – Antioxidants provide much-needed support for your elderly pup's immune system helping him to fight off diseases and illnesses.

Decreased levels of sodium and phosphorus – Lower phosphorus helps to maintain healthy kidney function and lower sodium levels keep your Poochon's blood pressure normal.

Omega-3 Fatty Acids – Healthy fats found in fish oil, nuts and plant oils help to decrease inflammation caused from arthritis and improve kidney and liver health.

Extra fiber – Many senior Poochons suffer from constipation, so extra fiber may help. However, too much fiber can cause other problems, so the best way to control constipation is making sure your dog gets enough exercise and adding a soluble source of fiber occasionally to his food such as canned, unsweetened sweet potatoes.

When choosing a senior dog food, it is important to consider your Poochon's individual needs, and recognize that these needs can change over time. So, just because one type of senior dog food is suitable for your dog now does not mean it will always be. The right dog food will have a direct impact on your dog's health, so take your time to research and talk to your vet to find the best diet for your faithful companion.

Look for a senior dog food made from premium quality ingredients such as human-grade organic lean red meats, and free of artificial preservatives. No matter how healthy your Poochon is, there is no need to put a strain on his immune system by feeding poor-quality, generic dog food with little to no nutritional value.

Transition your pooch slowly to a new senior dog food. It is best to start gradually by adding a small amount of the new food to their current food. Each day you can add a little more of the new food. Ideally, this process should take seven to ten days to completely switch your dog to the new food.

FUN FACT
Oldest Bichon Frise

Poochons live an average of 12 to 15 years, which is typical for breeds of this size. While no studies have been conducted to prove that this life span estimate is correct for Poochons, there have been several studies on the life span of Bichon Frise. The oldest Bichon Frise, according to these studies, lived to be 18 years old, while another lived to be 16 and a half!

Listen to your vets' recommendations especially if your dog has been diagnosed with a condition such as diabetes, kidney, liver or heart disease, arthritis, etc. Your vet will most likely recommend a prescription diet. While these diets often do not include the word "senior" in the title, they are formulated to manage disease conditions commonly seen in elderly dogs.

Exercise

As your Poochon ages, his mobility is going to decline. However, this does not mean he should not be getting any exercise. Actually, by helping your senior dog maintain an active lifestyle, you are decreasing his risks of geriatric ailments such as arthritis and muscle loss. Although, your old pup may not be chasing the ball as fast as he used to, there are still plenty of safe physical activities.

Here are a few suggestions to keep your senior Poochon active:

- Establish a regular exercise regime. The more active your Poochon is, the more agile he will feel even if it is several short walks a day instead of one or two long walks.
- Consider the climate before going for a trot around the block. Elderly dogs are more sensitive to extreme weather conditions. During the warmer months, take your Poochon for a walk in the cooler times of the day and, during the colder winter months, buy your dog a little jacket and booties.
- As your Poochon ages, he may lose his hearing and eyesight, so stick with the familiar walking routes. New surroundings may cause your furry friend to become anxious and confused.

Be sure to consult with your vet if your Poochon is receiving enough exercise, especially if he has a medical condition.

Never stop taking your Poochon for daily walks! Maybe your pooch will not be able to endure longer strolls but he will still be grateful to go for shorter walks. Walking gives your dog the opportunity to stretch his legs, sniff out his surroundings, and enjoy the fresh air.

Do not set the pace, instead let your Poochon set the pace. If your dog needs to sit or lie down for a minute or two, then let him rest.

Do not forget that indoor playtime is exercise. If the weather outside is too extreme, then keep your Poochon active by playing hide-and-seek inside.

Exercise helps keep your Poochon's mind stimulated, his weight healthy and his body agile. Regardless of your furry friend's physical limitations, there are plenty of appropriate exercises for your senior dog:

Walking – All dogs love going for walks, despite their age or health issues. Walking is one of the best low-impact exercises for your elderly dog as it improves his mental and physical health. Footing will impact your dog's walking ability, so grass and dirt are recommended surfaces. Avoid asphalt or rough gravel surfaces that may damage your dog's paws.

Swimming – Swimming is easy on your elderly dog's body, especially on the joints while providing a total body workout. An added bonus is your Poochon loves water and will be the happiest dog while he swims around the dog-friendly pool or lake. Swimming is often used as a form of physical therapy for dogs that have undergone major surgery for injuries.

There are plenty of other ideas to keep your senior dog active, such as playing fetch in the backyard or sniffing games that lead him to a treat. Give your Poochon time to follow his surroundings by sniffing out every shred of grass. However, whatever type of physical activity you choose for your dog – do not overdo it!

How much exercise is too much?

Every dog's physical tolerance levels vary depending on their weight, lifestyle, exercise history and overall health. Your Poochon may be pushing himself past his comfort zone just to please you. Here are a few tell-tale signs your dog pushed himself past his physical limitations:

Excessive drooling or panting – It is perfectly normal for your Poochon to pant a little after playing a game of fetch, however, excessive panting and drooling is a clear indication that he is dehydrated or overheated.

Reluctant to play – If your Poochon stops playing and wants to sit down, then he is telling you he is tired and needs to rest.

Limping or muscle atrophy – If your Poochon starts to favor his hind legs by limping while exercising – stop immediately! Observe your dog for the next twenty-four hours and if the limp does not go away, take him to see your vet as soon as possible.

Coughing or hacking – If your Poochon begins to cough or hack while exercising, it may be a sign of his tracheal collapsing or other health conditions. Repeated hacking can sound like your dog is honking. If your Poochon begins to make coughing or hacking sounds while exercising – stop immediately! If you notice the coughing noise returns every time that he exerts himself, consult with your vet.

It helps to keep an exercise journal of your Poochon's daily exercise regime and adjust his routine as needed. Whenever you notice your dog is experiencing pain or discomfort, slow down his workout. Do not hesitate to check in with your vet if you have any questions or concerns.

Old dog, new tricks

You have most likely heard the saying, "If you don't use it, you lose it!" Elderly people play sudoku, do crosswords or complete brain teasers to keep their minds sharp and alert. Your old faithful companion needs to keep learning new activities to keep his mind stimulated. When your dog is forced to focus on something, it tends to slow down cognitive degeneration.

Here are some ideas to keep your canine's mind sharp:

- Explore new places, such as parks, beaches or a ferry boat ride.
- Teach your Poochon new tricks or reinforce old ones.
- Reactivate old instincts with a game of tug of war.
- Take your old faithful companion swimming or, even better, to a local natural hot spring.
- Play a short game of fetch or hide-and-seek.
- Introduce new toys or games that involve sniffing out a yummy treat.

Grooming

Grooming is essential throughout your Poochon's life but even more so as he gets older. Grooming sessions are an excellent opportunity to observe any changes in your dog's overall health, as many underlying health issues are revealed through the health of his skin and coat. Fur can begin to thin and, skin irritation, new growths or lumps may start to appear.

One of the best gifts you can give your aging Poochon is daily grooming as it keeps him looking and feeling his best. Plus, he will drink up the extra attention from you. Your dog is never too old to be pampered!

Typically, elderly dogs who loved getting groomed in their younger years, suddenly start to resist the process due to joint pain. Senior dogs may squirm and bark to vocalize their objections to being groomed. However, at the end of the grooming session, your Poochon will be prancing around like he was still a puppy!

Your older Poochon will thank you for his grooming session. A warm bath will relieve those itchy sections your dog is no longer able to reach. Plus, your Poochon will drink up the extra attention and the treats during the grooming and afterwards. Nothing is more satisfying to see than your freshly groomed old companion swagger away feeling completely renewed and refreshed.

If you prefer to take your Poochon to a professional groomer, avoid using a discount service that may neglect your dog. Not every groomer has the ability or the patience to deal with your faithful old companion's aches and pains, so choose carefully. Look for a groomer who has experience with grooming geriatric dogs.

If you decide to groom your Poochon at home, be sure to review the detailed instructions in chapter 11 of this book and take into consideration the following suggestions to adapt the process to your old friend. These tips can go a long way in ensuring your elderly dog will receive the level of care and respect he deserves.

Whether you decide to groom your elderly Poochon at home or use a professional groomer, consider the following suggestions beforehand:

Keep sessions short – Lengthy grooming sessions can expose your older dog to unnecessary discomfort, pain and stress. Many reputable groomers with experience grooming geriatric dogs will schedule multiple grooming sessions instead of one. For example, the first session may include a bath and the following week a haircut and brushing.

Watch for signs of discomfort – Your older dog will communicate his discomfort through body language or by vocalizing. If you notice your Poochon whimpering, squirming, shivering or even growling, then you need to stop the grooming session. Let your dog take a short rest or find a more comfortable position. If your Poochon becomes agitated or stressed, then discontinue the session and continue another day.

Understand your dog's limitations – It is more than likely your senior Poochon may not be able to handle the same grooming regimen as when he was younger. Pressure sores and benign fatty tumors mean your dog's coat cannot be trimmed as short as usual. Or perhaps if your Poochon has poor eyesight, clipping too close to his face may cause him anxiety.

Bathing – If you decide to bathe your elderly Poochon at home, there are a few precautions you can take to ensure his well-being and comfort. When bathing your dog, place a non-skid mat in the bottom of the basin or tub to secure his footing. Make sure the water is warm enough that your Poochon is not shivering during the bath. Often, geriatric dogs need a special shampoo to treat dry skin or other conditions.

After thoroughly rinsing out the shampoo, dry your dog with warm, fluffy towels. Before using the blow dryer, let your Poochon shake himself off. Never use the blow dryer on the hottest setting. Instead, use the cool setting. Be sure to get your old dog as dry as possible, as water trapped close to the skin may cause hot spots.

Brushing – Before you start brushing your Poochon, inspect the brush to make sure it's in good condition. If the brush's teeth are bent or broken, it is best to discard it and get a new one, as the teeth can scratch an older dog's thin, vulnerable skin or damage his coat.

Unfortunately, arthritis and joint pain may make it difficult for him to stand in the same position for long periods of time. Place a blanket on the floor and have your Poochon lie on his side while being brushed. Despite common belief, matted, tangled hair does not provide your dog with extra insulation as much as clean, tangle-free hair will.

While brushing your Poochon, be on the lookout for bare patches and brittle hair. This may be an indication of health conditions. Also, use your fingers to feel for any new lumps, warts or sores on your dog's skin. If you notice anything suspicious, consult with your vet.

Nail trimming – Your elderly Poochon will need his nails trimmed more frequently than when he was younger. If your old dog suffers from arthritis or joint problems, it is even more reason to keep his nails trimmed, as the nail length affects your dog's posture and can force him to torque his spine, causing additional discomfort. In the past, his long walks on the sidewalk naturally kept his nails trimmed, but nowadays because of his shorter, golden strolls, he needs some extra help to keep his nails short.

Sanitary areas – The glands and groin area are normally cleaned by your dog daily, but with old age he may need some help. Regular trimming of the groin area will prevent any fecal matter or urine from getting trapped. Typically, all dogs express their anal glands when they defecate. But smaller breeds such as the Poochon may need help to express their anal glands as they age.

Saying Goodbye

For every person who loves and shares their life with a Poochon, the dreaded and inevitable day will come when you have to ask yourself whether or not to intervene in how or when your beloved four-pawed friend's life must come to an end. The very thought of having to say goodbye to your best friend for the last time is definitely heart-wrenching.

More often than not, when we start to observe signs that our dog is dying, we start second guessing ourselves or even go into denial. This often causes our beloved dogs to suffer far longer than they should have. The question is how do you know? When is the right time to put your best friend to a forever sleep?

Tell-tale signs your dog is dying

Prolonged lethargy or disinterest - One of the most common signs of the dying process is finding your dog lying in the same spot (often not where he would normally rest), barely acknowledging you or other family members. Dogs may become lethargic due to other health conditions, but if the veterinarian has ruled this out and the lethargy lasts for more than a few days, then maybe it is time to consider saying goodbye.

Stops eating or drinking - Another classic sign something is wrong with your Poochon is when you offer him the tastiest treat imaginable and he refuses to even sniff it. Often at this point, the dog will stop drinking water, as his organs are starting to shut down. Try keeping your dog hydrated by giving him water using a dropper or turkey baster, but if he still refuses to swallow, there is not much you can do at this point. Be sure to rule out other health conditions with your vet.

Lack of coordination - The next sign is when your dog begins to lose balance and motor control.

When your elderly Poochon tries to stand up, he may be very wobbly or disoriented. Or he could shake or convulse while lying down. In this case, make your dog as comfortable as possible and remove any objects he could knock over if he tries to stand up. Note: Saying goodbye to your dog means protecting him, creating a safe area for him, and providing whatever help he needs.

Incontinence – When a dog is dying, often he will not even move from the spot to relieve himself even if he has diarrhea. This is an indication that your dog's organs are starting to shut down. During this stage, make sure you keep him and his bed clean and dry.

Labored breathing – As heartbreaking as it sounds, towards the end, many dogs display labored breathing. Your dog's breathing may become difficult, with lengthy gasps between each breath. This is an extremely hard moment, as you know at this point your dog is suffering.

Seeking comfort – This is one of the hardest moments, as despite your dog's quickly deteriorating health, he looks for comfort from his people – from you. During these final hours, be with your dog, reassuring him of your love and affection.

Making the decision

The signs above are not always consistent, as some dogs suddenly pass away in their sleep without any indications and other dogs exhibit even more signs. Part of preparing to say goodbye to your Poochon is realizing you may have to make the difficult decision for your dog by intervening. Be sure to talk over the decision with your significant other and come to a mutual agreement.

Once you come to a decision of intervening due to your dog's suffering, discuss the options with your vet.

Veterinarians are required to follow a set of guidelines called the "Humane Euthanasia Protocol," whether the euthanasia is performed inside of the clinic or in the tranquility of your own house. The entire process is painless and stress-free for your Poochon. The Humane Euthanasia Protocol is considered to be the most humane way to put your dog to sleep.

The Humane Euthanasia Protocol:

1. The veterinarian will inject your Poochon with a pain tranquilizer.
2. Once your dog is relaxed and sedated, then your vet will insert an IV to administrate the euthanasia solution.
3. The vet will leave you alone with your dog for a few minutes for any final goodbyes, then return to administer the final drug to stop his heart.

However, in certain parts of the United States veterinarians are not required by law to adhere to the Humane Euthanasia Protocol. Instead, they practice a quicker and more affordable method to stop the animal's heart with a single injection of barbiturates. Barbiturates cause the animal's central nervous system to slow down causing a painful death. This type of euthanasia is not humane, as it is not pain-free, causing the animal short-term distress and anxiety.

Ensure your veterinarian applies the Humane Euthanasia Protocol on your dog. If not look for another veterinarian who will.

Most dogs are euthanized inside of the veterinary clinic, but many vets will make house calls. If your vet is unable to make house calls, you can find an extensive list of reputable veterinarians throughout the United States and Canada at the In-Home Pet Euthanasia Directory.

Here is a quick overview of pros and cons of getting your Poochon euthanized at home vs. at the clinic.

At-home euthanasia may be the right choice for you if:

- Your Poochon is too sick to be transported comfortably to the veterinary clinic.
- You personally feel more comfortable with grieving at home.
- Car trips or visits to the veterinary clinic cause your dog anxiety and stress.
- Money is not an issue, as at-home procedures cost more.
- Vet clinic euthanasia may be the right choice for you if:
- You want your usual vet to perform the procedure, but they are unable to perform house calls.
- You prefer a more neutral environment for the procedure.
- Your dog is still mobile enough to be comfortably transported in your car.
- Cost is a concern.

Whether you decide on euthanasia at-home or at the veterinary clinic is a very personal decision. There is no right or wrong answer.

The cost of clinical euthanasia can be between $80 to $350 depending on where you live. The cost of at-home euthanasia can cost between $300 to $800. The higher cost may include add-ons, such as cremations, funeral services or getting the vet to take an impression of your dog's paw to cast into a memento.

It is highly recommended you pay for the euthanasia before the procedure as emotions can be running high when the procedure is final, and the last thing you need is to relive the heartbreak by receiving the bill later. When it is all over, you can request the veterinary clinic to dispose of your dog for an extra cost. Some clinics offer a cremation or a professional burial service at a nearby pet cemetery.

Take your time grieving your Poochon and come to terms with your loss. Everybody does it in their own way. Saying goodbye to your Poochon does not mean forgetting about him. With time, you may start thinking about opening up your heart to another dog.

> *"How lucky am I to have something that makes saying goodbye so hard."*
>
> Winnie the Pooh

Printed in Great Britain
by Amazon